INSTANT POT

COOKBOOK

Ultimate Pressure Cooking Guide for Busy People

Jamie Jensen

Copyright Legal Information

Introduction

Welcome to Instant Pot Cookbook – Ultimate Pressure Cooking Guide for Busy People. The recipes in this cookbook is curated and designed for everyday cooking without the fuss and muss of the age old question *"What's for dinner?"*

It's not easy to run a household and after a long day of work your creative juices might be too drained to come up with meal ideas. In this recipe book you will find delicious meals that could easily be prepared and cooked in your Pressure Cooker hassle free. With this little cookbook you will be inspired to love your kitchen again and make meal planning a breeze. It is a collection of recipes of your favorite home-cooked meals that will keep your family full and smiling.

In here, you will find recipes for your favorite meat and seafood dishes, curries, chilies and pastas! If you are feeling more adventurous and need a quick pick-me-up then the Butter Chicken recipe or the Jumbo Shrimp Curry might be just what you need on a Monday night. No matter how you are feeling, there is a recipe to suit your every mood and taste bud!

The recipe collection are also very versatile and would make great lunches, weekend dinners and even holiday feasts that will surely impress your relatives and in-laws!

We sincerely hope you enjoy this Instant Pot Cookbook as much as we did cooking our way through all these great recipes.

Disclaimer: Cook times and Prep times are suggested times based on trial and preferences. The cook times are also recommendations from Instant Pot manuals that have been adjusted by our team. We have provided "Notes" sections in the recipes for you to add in your own personal tips and tricks on how to make *your* perfect dinner entrée.

Table of Contents

Measurements

The Pasta Measurements are for servings of 2 people

LONG PASTAS	DRY PASTA Measured with Hand	COOKED PASTA Measured in Cups
Angel Hair	2 to 3inches (circumference)	2 cups
Fettuccine	2 to 3inches (circumference)	2 cups
Linguine	2 to 3inches (circumference)	2 cups
Spaghetti	2 to 3inches (circumference)	2 cups
Thin Spaghetti	2 to 3inches (circumference)	2 cups

The Pasta Measurements are for servings of 2 people

SHORT PASTAS	DRY PASTA Measured in Cups
Macaroni Elbows	2 cups
Penne	2 cups
Rigatoni	2 cups
Rotini	2 cups
Farfalle	2 cups
Fusilli	2 cups

Canned Soups and Sauces used in this cookbook
- The sizes used in this recipe is 14 oz. (Equivalent to 1 and ¾ cups)

Frozen Bagged Vegetables used in this cookbook
- The sizes used is 14 oz. this typically feeds about 4 people (or 2 really hungry teenagers)

Optimum Servings for the recipes used in this cookbook
- The ideal portion size in this recipe cookbook is between 4 to 8 servings. The reason behind this is that to get the most use out of your pressure cooker and the recipes is to not over crowd your ingredients.

CONVERSION TABLE

LENGTH			WEIGHT		TEMPERATURE	
INCHES	DECIMAL	MM	IMPERIAL	METRIC	FAHRENHEIT	CELSIUS
1/16	0,06	1,59	1/2 oz	15 g	5	-15
1/8	0,13	3,18	1 oz	29 g	10	-12
3/16	0,19	4,76	2 oz	57 g	25	-4
1/4	0,25	6,35	3 oz	85 g	50	10
5/16	0,31	7,94	4 oz	113 g	100	37
3/8	0,38	9,53	5 oz	141 g	150	65
7/16	0,44	11,11	6 oz	170 g	200	93
1/2	0,50	12,70	8 oz	227 g	250	121
9/16	0,56	14,29	10 oz	283 g	300	150
5/8	0,63	15,88	12 oz	340 g	325	160
11/16	0,69	17,46	13 oz	369 g	350	180
3/4	0,75	19,05	14 oz	397 g	375	190
13/16	0,81	20,64	15 oz	425 g	400	200
7/8	0,88	22,23	1 lb	453 g	425	220
15/16	0,94	23,81	1½ lb	680 g	450	230
1	1,00	25,40	2,2 lb	1 kg	500	260

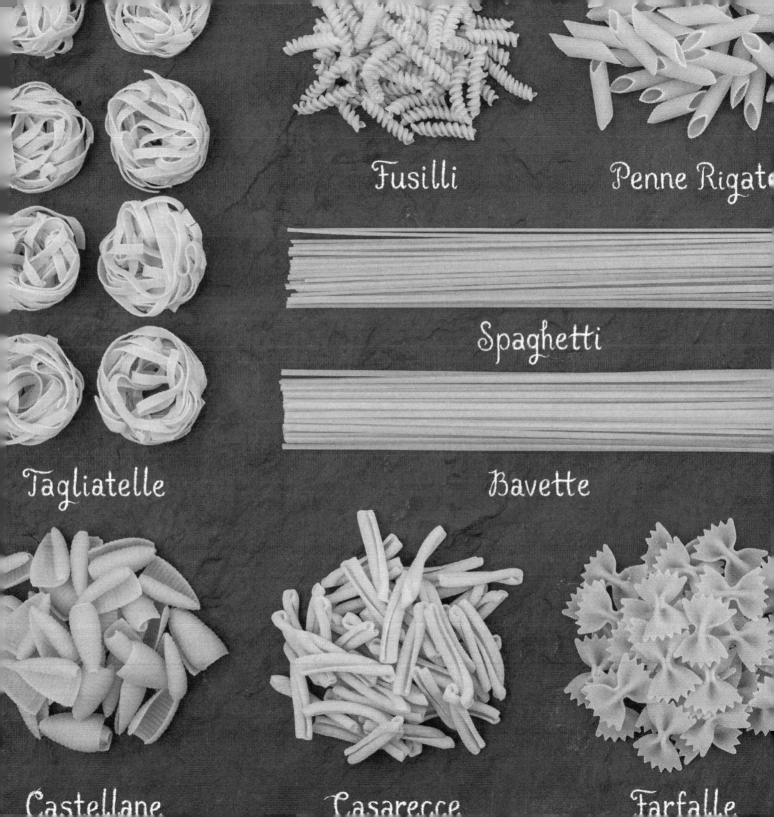

Fusilli

Penne Rigate

Spaghetti

Bavette

Tagliatelle

Castellane

Casarecce

Farfalle

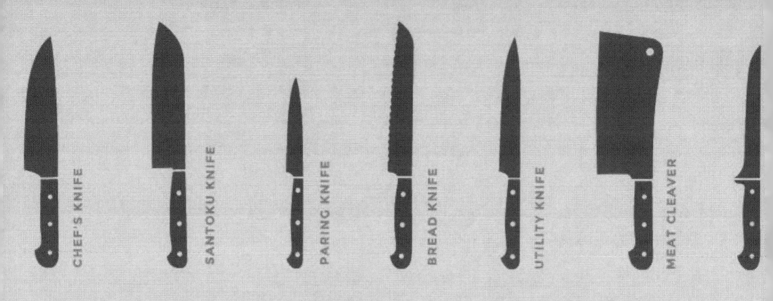

Cutting Essentials – Knife Diagram

Knife Guide

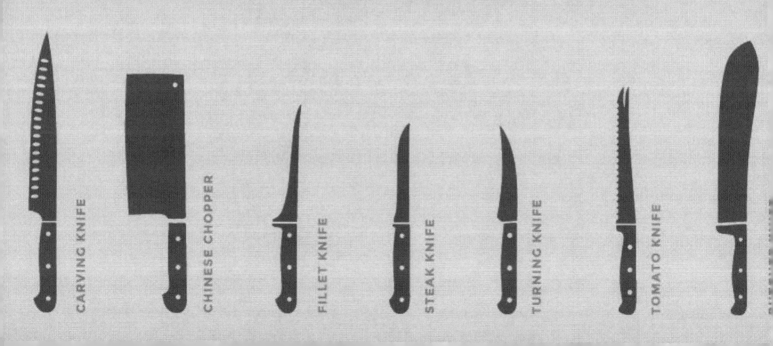

Top 3 thing to know about your Instant Pot

1. Read the Manual and go through the buttons

- Sauté function – use the Sauté button to sauté in the pressure cooking pot with the lid off. You can also press Sauté and the Adjust button once (more) for browning.
- Keep Warm/Cancel Button – Use this button to cancel a function or turn off your pressure cooker.
- Manual button is an all-purpose button. Use the manual button if a recipe says to pressure cook on High pressure for a specific number of minutes.
- Slow Cooker – defaults to a 4 hour slow cook time. Use the adjust button to slow cook on low (190-201°F), normal (194-205°F) or high (199-210°F).
- Pressure – switches between low and high pressure.
- Timer – is for delayed cooking. You need to select a cooking function first, make any adjustments, and then press the timer button.

2. No canning in your Instant Pot

A frequently asked question around the internet is whether or not you can pressure-can in the Instant Pot – and the answer is simply no. The pressure cooker is regulated by a pressure sensor instead of a thermometer. The USDA, has not tested the Instant Pot for food safety in pressure-canning.

3. Consider getting a second stainless steel insert

Your Instant Pot comes with one stainless steel insert, but it's nice to have one available to use while the other one is in the dishwasher. Also, with the second one you can quickly change settings on the Instant Pot and make a couple different dishes.

How to Clean your Instant Pot

Ingredients

- Vinegar
- Gentle Dish soap

Equipment

- Cotton or microfiber cloth
- Small scrub brush

1. Always unplug any appliance before cleaning. It's also a great time to check the cord for any damage or needed repairs.

2. Separate lid and interior pot from housing and clean, keep in mind the housing has electrical components and should NEVER be immersed in water. Wipe exterior of housing to remove crumbs and tough stains. Use a small brush to remove dried food residue in the recessed area of the housing unit.

3. Hand-wash lid with warm, soapy water and then wipe dry with soft cloth.

4. Remove the steam-release handle by pulling it off gently to check for food particles. Remove the anti-block shield from the underside of the lid to wipe the steam valve clean, but NEVER remove the steam valve.

5. Remove the silicone ring anchoring the float valve and clean both portions; reattach when dry. Always inspect the float valve to make sure it can move up and down easily without obstruction.

6. Remove sealing ring. The silicone sealing ring should be removed periodically to remove lingering smells and to inspect for damage. If you notice cracking, leaking, or deformation of the sealing ring, you should replace it. The silicone ring can be washed in the dishwasher or soaked in vinegar first to remove odors. The sealing ring should always be clean and well-seated before use to ensure a proper seal during pressure cooking.

7. Wash the inner pot and steam rack. The inner pot and steam rack may be hand-washed or washed in the dishwasher.

8. DO NOT use any type of steel wool or hard brushes on the surface of your Instant Pot or inner pot. It will damage and scratch the surface if used.

9. Reassemble. Make sure all parts are securely reattached to ensure the proper seal. Double-check that the silicone sealing ring, anti-block shield, and float valve weren't forgotten! Then get back to making some dinner magic.

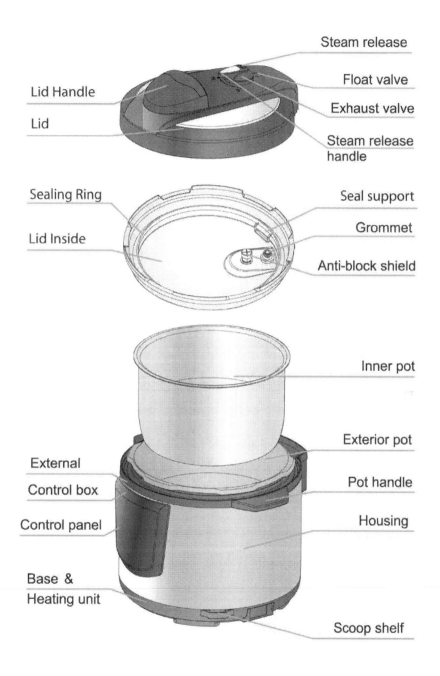

Steam release

Float valve

Lid Handle

Exhaust valve

Lid

Steam release handle

Sealing Ring

Seal support

Grommet

Lid Inside

Anti-block shield

Inner pot

Exterior pot

External

Control box

Pot handle

Control panel

Housing

Base & Heating unit

Scoop shelf

Pressure Release Guide and Terminology

It's always a good idea to read the manual of your Instant Pot/Pressure Cooker. The following is a simple guide to get you familiar with the Pressure Release of the Instant Pot, followed by a list of terminology that will be useful when you start cooking with your Instant Pot.

Quick Pressure Release

This type of release is used to quickly stop the cooking process and prevents overcooking more delicate foods such as leafy green vegetables and certain types of seafood that require very short cooking time. This method is also slightly messier in terms of lots of steam and liquid gets splattered on the roof of your Instant Pot lid and may even spill a little into the Exterior Pot. If you use the Quick Pressure Release often, then it is best to clean your Instant Pot at a more regular cleaning interval.

Natural Pressure Release

This is a much cleaner method for releasing pressure in your instant pot, and this is the **method used** in the recipes in this cookbook collection. The Natural Pressure Release gradually releases the pressure inside your Instant Pot, therefore less movement and your foods, such as soups, sauces and meats come out cleaner and more intact.

- **QR** – Quick Release Open valve & release steam quickly

- **NR** – Natural Release Leave valve closed & allow pressure to drop on its own.

- **HP** – High Pressure

- **Sauté** – Use the Sauté button to brown and simmer with the pressure cooking lid off.

- **Keep Warm/Cancel** – Use this button to cancel a function or turn off your pressure cooker.

- **Manual** – An all-purpose button. Use this to pressure cook on High pressure for specific number of minutes. Use the "+" and "-" buttons to increase or decrease the cooking time.

What's in Your Spice Rack?

Basil
Fresh basil is used in pastas, pizzas and stews. It is also a main ingredient in pesto.

Sea Salt
Used in roasting and as a brine for a variety of meats and seafood.

Cumin
Mainly used for highly spiced foods and is a popular spice in Indian, and Mexican cooking. It goes great with stews and grilled meats, especially lamb and chicken dishes.

Clove
Used in Asian and Middle Eastern cuisines in curries and marinades.

Nutmeg
A fragrant spice used mostly in baking and desserts, also a favorite in eggnog and other European cuisines.

Bay Leaf
This aromatic spice goes great in meat sauces, and thick pasta sauces. It's also a favorite in hearty stews and stocks.

Dried/Fresh Garlic
Aromatic and delicious in just about anything. Dried garlic is very easy to use to season and marinate meats, fish and vegetables.

Paprika
Favorite spice used to season rice, stews and sausages.

Black Pepper
Popular spice used to season foods and is a staple in every kitchen.

Coriander
Dried coriander seeds are a staple in South East Asian cooking and is found in garam masala and other Indian curries. The fresh coriander leaves are used mostly as a garnish or added to broths to give it a more citrus note.

Cayenne Pepper
Common spice found in hot sauces and is usually sprinkled onto sandwiches or pastas to add a spicy flavor.

Sage
Savory and peppery, it is also a staple in Italian cooking and goes great with meat and fish dishes as well as on grilled vegetables.

Curcuma/Turmeric

Also known as turmeric and is found in a lot of South East Asian cuisines such as Thai curries and dishes.

Ginger

Whether it's fresh or ground into a powder, ginger is an essential spice for cooking seafood (it helps minimize the 'fishy-ness' of the seafood) and is a staple in a lot of curries and Asian cooking.

Cinnamon

Mostly used in baking and in coffees and teas, it's a wonderful spice to add aroma to your stews and desserts.

Chili

Fresh and dried chilies are used in a variety of dishes, and adds a spicy kick to meats, vegetables and even desserts.

Oregano

Oregano is a common herb in Italian cuisines and go great in pizza sauce and grilled vegetables, meat and fish.

Saffron

Saffron has a delicious honey and grassy notes to it and is a beloved spice of Asian and Middle Eastern cuisines. It's commonly used in baking and flavoring rice and pastas.

Create Your Own Spice Mix

Ingredients	Date of Spice Mix

Beef
Dinners

Beef Cuts

Parts

1 - Chuck	5 - Short Loin	9 - Top Sirloin
2 - Brisket	6 - Flank	10 - Bottom Sirloin
3 - Rib	7 - Sirloin	11 - Round
4 - Plate	8 - Tenderloin	12 - Shanks

Parts

1 - Chuck	5 - Short Loin	9 - Top Sirloin
2 - Brisket	6 - Flank	10 - Bottom Sirloin
3 - Rib	7 - Sirloin	11 - Round
4 - Plate	8 - Tenderloin	12 - Shanks

Easy Short Ribs

COOK TIME
15-20 MIN
PREP TIME
10 MIN
SERVINGS
4 SERVINGS

INGREDIENTS

- 2 lbs. short ribs
- 1 tablespoon oil
- 4 tablespoons soy sauce
- 2 tablespoons brown sugar
- 3 tablespoons honey
- 3 Cloves garlic, minced
- ¼ cup ketchup
- 2 tablespoons minced onion
- 2 tablespoons rice vinegar
- 1 teaspoon sriracha

PREPARATION

1. Combine all the sauce ingredients in a bowl and give it a quick mix (the following ingredients below)
- 1 tablespoon oil
- 4 tablespoons soy sauce
- 2 tablespoons brown sugar
- 3 tablespoons honey
- 3 Cloves garlic, minced
- ¼ cup ketchup
- 2 tablespoons minced onion
- 2 tablespoons rice vinegar
- teaspoon sriracha

2. Heat the oil in the pressure cooker until very hot and add the ribs and drizzle the mixed sauce ingredients all over the ribs.

3. Lock lid and cook on High for 20 minutes. Set timer. Once timer goes off, release pressure naturally and serve with your favorite salad.

Grammy's Beef Stroganoff

COOK TIME
20 MIN
PREP TIME
10 MIN
SERVINGS
6-8 SERVINGS

INGREDIENTS

- 2 pounds of beef round steak cut into one inch pieces
- 1 large onion diced
- 2 cups of sliced white mushrooms
- 1 cup of tomato sauce
- ¼ dried parsley flakes

- 1 tablespoon minced fresh garlic
- 1 cup beef broth
- 1 tablespoon butter
- 1 tablespoon olive oil
- Salt and Pepper to taste
- 1/3 cup of sour cream

PREPARATION

1. In a mixing bowl add your beef and season with two small pinch of salt and pepper. In another small mixing bowl whisk together the following ingredients:

- 1 cup of tomato sauce
- ¼ dried parsley flakes
- 1 tablespoon minced fresh garlic
- 1 cup beef broth

2. Set your pressure cooker to medium and add in the butter and olive oil, once hot, quickly brown your beef for 2 minutes.

3. Add in the diced onion and white mushrooms and give it a gentle stir.

4. Then add in your whisked ingredients and cover with lid and lock it in place and cook on High for 20 minutes. Set timer.

5. Once timer goes off, release pressure naturally and give it a gentle stir. Serve over pasta with a dollop of sour cream.

Classic Roast and Potatoes

COOK TIME
45 MIN
PREP TIME
15 MIN
SERVINGS
6 SERVINGS

INGREDIENTS

- 1 (3 to 4 pound) boneless beef chuck-eye roast, trimmed
- Sea salt and pepper to taste
- 1 tablespoon olive oil
- 1 onion, finely chopped
- 1 shallot, minced

- 2 tablespoons tomato paste
- ½ ounce dried porcini mushrooms, rinsed and minced
- 2 cups beef broth
- 2 pounds small Yukon Gold potatoes

PREPARATION

1. Season beef with salt and pepper and brown in pressure cooker with the oil. Brown each side for 8 to 10 minutes. Then set aside on a platter.

2. Add the onions and shallot into the cooked oil in the pot and cook until softened 2 minutes.

3. Add: tomato paste, mushrooms, potatoes, beef broth and the beef loaf in the center of the pressure cooker.

4. Lock lid and cook on High and set timer for 45 minutes.

5. When timer goes off, turn off pressure cooker and release pressure naturally. Transfer everything from the pot onto a serving plate.

6. While the beef is resting, strain juices through a sieve and return it to the pressure cooker and sauté the juices with some flour to create a gravy.

Amazing Sloppy Joes

COOK TIME
30 MIN
PREP TIME
15 MIN
SERVINGS
4-6 SERVINGS

INGREDIENTS

- 2 lbs. ground beef
- 1 cup ketchup
- 1 large can of stewed tomatoes
- ½ cup chopped red peppers and onions
- 2 teaspoon minced garlic
- 1 teaspoon onion powder

- 1 tablespoon Worcestershire
- 2 tablespoons brown sugar
- 2 tablespoons chili powder
- 1 tablespoon yellow mustard
- A Squirt of sriracha
- Salt and pepper to taste

PREPARATION

1. Sauté on how and quickly brown the ground beef with minced garlic and onion powder and a drizzle of sesame oil. 2 minutes.

2. Stir the rest of the ingredients together in a bowl and pour it over the ground beef and mix well before closing the lid.

3. Once everything is incorporated, lock lid and cook on High for 30 minutes. Set timer.

4. Once timer goes off, release pressure naturally and remove lid, serve with your favorite bun and sides.

Notes

Shredded Beef Roast with Carrots

COOK TIME
60 MIN
PREP TIME
10 MIN
SERVINGS
2-4 SERVINGS

INGREDIENTS

- 2-pound boneless beef chuck shoulder roast (No substitutions)
- 1-2 pounds carrots, peeled and chopped into chunks
- 3 tablespoons sesame oil
- 1 cup beef stock
- 1 cup of red wine

- 2 tablespoons Worcestershire sauce
- 1 teaspoon sea salt
- ½ teaspoon white pepper
- ½ teaspoon mustard powder
- ½ teaspoon oregano
- ½ teaspoon garlic or onion powder

PREPARATION

1. Season your beef with the sea salt and white pepper, make sure you rub it into the meat thoroughly. Set aside.

2. In a mixing bowl whisk together the wet ingredients with the dried ingredients. Then place your beef chuck in the center of the pressure cooker. Surround the meat with the carrots, and pour your whisked mixture over the meat and carrots.

3. Lock lid and cook on High for 60 minutes. Set timer. Once timer goes off, release pressure naturally. Check that the meat is tender enough to shred with a fork. If not, you can cook on High for another 10 minutes.

4. To serve, shred the meat in the pot, and serve over a bed of rice or Asian noodles. The carrots would also be very soft, adding to the sauce of the meat.

Notes

Grandpa's Savory Meatballs

COOK TIME
15 MIN
PREP TIME
10 MIN
SERVINGS
4-6 SERVINGS

INGREDIENTS

- 1 medium onion, finely chopped
- 2 cloves minced garlic
- ½ cup plain dried bread crumbs
- ½ teaspoon dried oregano
- ½ teaspoon dried parsley
- ¼ teaspoon black pepper

- 2 teaspoons salt
- 1 tablespoon olive oil
- 1 large egg
- 1 pound mixed/ground beef meat
- 1 jar of your favorite tomato sauce
- 2 cups water

PREPARATION

1. In a large mixing bowl add the following ingredients to your ground beef:
- 1 medium onion, finely chopped
- 2 cloves minced garlic
- ½ cup plain dried bread crumbs
- ½ teaspoon dried oregano
- ½ teaspoon dried parsley
- ¼ teaspoon black pepper
- 2 teaspoons salt
- 1 tablespoon olive oil

2. Mix with your hands until everything is incorporated, then crack your egg into the mixture and mix until the egg is incorporated into the meet and seasonings. Set aside the mixture.

3. In your pressure cooker add the jar of tomato sauce and water and let it heat up on medium in 'sauté' mode.

4. Place your meat mixture next to the pressure cooker and start making meatballs – make sure you make them the same size and place each one of the meatballs into your sauce. Keep layering the meatballs into your pressure cooker until you run out of mixture. Close and lock the lid of your pressure cooker and cook for 15 minutes on high. Set timer.

5. Once timer goes off release pressure naturally and serve with your favorite pasta or jasmine rice. It goes great with a crusty baguette too and the sauce is excellent for dipping.

Maple Smoked Brisket

COOK TIME
40 MIN
PREP TIME
10 MIN
SERVINGS
2-4 SERVINGS

INGREDIENTS

- 2 pound beef brisket, cut into 2 pieces
- 2 tablespoon maple syrup
- 1 tablespoon of brown sugar
- 1 tablespoon smoked sea salt
- 1 teaspoon black pepper
- 1 teaspoon mustard powder
- 1 teaspoon onion powder
- 1 teaspoon smoked paprika
- 1 tablespoon of olive oil
- 2 cups beef stock
- 2 fresh thyme sprigs

PREPARATION

1. Place your brisket in a mixing bowl and coat it with the following ingredients:
- 2 tablespoon maple syrup
- 1 tablespoon of brown sugar
- 1 tablespoon smoked sea salt
- 1 teaspoon black pepper
- 1 teaspoon mustard powder
- 1 teaspoon onion powder
- 1 teaspoon smoked paprika

2. Set your pressure cooker to "Sauté" and add olive oil and brown your brisket on both sides 2 minutes each side.

3. Once browned leave your brisket in the pressure cooker and add the beef stock and thyme to your brisket and cook on High. Set timer to 40 minutes.

4. Once timer goes off release pressure naturally. Remove brisket from liquid.

5. Serve with vegetables, mash potatoes or jasmine rice.

Vietnamese Beef Stew

COOK TIME
30 MIN
PREP TIME
10 MIN
SERVINGS
4-6 SERVINGS

INGREDIENTS

- 2 ½ pounds stew-cut beef cut into small chunks
- 3 large cloves garlic, minced
- 3 tablespoon minced fresh ginger
- 1 ½ tsp brown sugar
- 1 teaspoon ground black pepper
- 3 tablespoon fish sauce
- 3 tablespoon tomato paste
- 3 stalks lemongrass cut into 3-inch lengths

- 2 whole star anise
- 3 cups beef broth
- 3 cups of coconut water
- 2 cups of water
- 1 medium onion chopped
- 4 large carrots, peeled and cut into chunks
- 3 large potatoes, peeled and cut into chunks
- ¼ cup coarsely chopped fresh cilantro leaves

PREPARATION

1. In a mixing bowl marinate beef with following and set aside:

- 3 large cloves garlic, minced
- 3 tablespoon minced fresh ginger
- 1 ½ tsp brown sugar
- 1 teaspoon ground black pepper
- 3 tablespoon fish sauce
- 3 tablespoon tomato paste

2. Heat pressure cooker on High, add a drizzle of olive oil and quickly brown the beef chunks.

3. Then add the following to your pressure cooker:

- 3 stalks lemongrass cut into 3-inch lengths
- 2 whole star anise
- 3 cups beef broth
- 3 cups of coconut water
- 2 cups of water
- 1 medium onion chopped
- 4 large carrots, peeled and cut into chunks
- 3 large potatoes, peeled and cut into chunks
- ¼ cup coarsely chopped fresh cilantro leaves

4. Once you've added the rest of your ingredients then lock lid and cook on High for 20 minutes. Set timer.

5. Once timer goes off release pressure naturally and check for softness of the carrots.

6. You should be able to easily stick a fork through, if not you can cook for another 5 minutes.

7. Serve with Asian noodles and a squeeze of fresh lime or dip with crusty baguette.

Serving Tip:

For a more authentic style, serve with fresh basil leaves and raw bean sprouts. Hot chili oil and hoisin sauce make a great addition as dipping sauces for the noodles.

Storage Tip:

The stew can be made in larger batches, you can double to recipe. If you do decide to make a larger batch, separate the stew into 2 servings and store them either in air tight containers or freezer friendly Ziploc bags. The stew can be kept in the freezer for up to 3 weeks.

Notes

Mexican Style Short Ribs

COOK TIME
15-20 MIN
PREP TIME
10 MIN
SERVINGS
4 SERVINGS

INGREDIENTS

- 2 lbs. short ribs
- 1 tablespoon sesame oil
- 4 tablespoons soy sauce
- 2 tablespoons brown sugar
- 3 tablespoons honey
- 3 Cloves garlic, minced

- 2 tablespoon paprika
- 2 tablespoons minced onion
- 2 tablespoon minced green chili
- 2 tablespoons red wine
- 1 teaspoon sriracha

PREPARATION

1. Combine all the sauce ingredients in a bowl and give it a quick mix (the following ingredients below)
- 1 tablespoon sesame oil
- 4 tablespoons soy sauce
- 2 tablespoons brown sugar
- 3 tablespoons honey

- 3 Cloves garlic, minced
- 2 tablespoon paprika
- 2 tablespoons minced onion
- 2 tablespoon minced green chili
- 2 tablespoons red wine
- 1 teaspoon sriracha

2. Heat a drizzle of olive oil in the pressure cooker until very hot and add the short ribs and sauté for 2 minutes, then coat the ribs with the mixed sauce. Once fully mixed, lock lid and cook on High for 20 minutes. Set timer.

3. Once timer goes off, release pressure naturally and serve the short ribs with your favorite salad.

Mongolian Beef

COOK TIME
15-20 MIN
PREP TIME
15 MIN
SERVINGS
6 SERVINGS

INGREDIENTS

- 2 pounds flank steak, cut into 1/4" strips
- 1 tablespoon vegetable oil
- 4 cloves garlic, minced or pressed
- ½ cup soy sauce
- ½ cup water
-

- 2/3 cup dark brown sugar
- ½ teaspoon minced fresh ginger
- 2 tablespoon cornstarch
- 3 tablespoons water
- 3 green onions, sliced into 1-inch pieces

PREPARATION

1. Season beef with salt and pepper. Put oil in the pressure cooker and brown on High. When oil begins to sizzle, brown meat in batches until all meat is browned - do not crowd. Transfer meat to a plate when browned.

2. Add the garlic and sauté 1 minute. Add soy sauce, ½ cup water, brown sugar, and ginger. Stir to combine.

3. Add browned beef and any accumulated juices. Cook on High. Set timer for 12 minutes.

4. When timer goes off, release pressure naturally, then combine the cornstarch and 3 tablespoons water, whisking until smooth. Add cornstarch mixture to the sauce in the pot stirring constantly. Bring back to a boil and add in green onions. Stir for another minute and serve over jasmine rice.

Notes

Classic Beef and Broccoli

COOK TIME
15-20 MIN
PREP TIME
15 MIN
SERVINGS
6 SERVINGS

INGREDIENTS

- 1 (3 to 4 pound) boneless beef chuck-eye cut into small chunks
- Sea salt and pepper to taste
- 1 tablespoon olive oil
- 1 onion, finely chopped
- 1 shallot, minced
- 2 cups beef broth
- 2 pounds broccoli stems trimmed and cut into chunks (do not cut it too small)

PREPARATION

1. Season beef with salt and pepper and brown in pressure cooker with the oil. Brown each side for 2 minutes. Then set aside on a platter.

2. Add the onions and shallot into the cooked oil in the pot and cook until softened about 1 minute.

3. Add the beef broth and the beef in the center of the pressure cooker. Lock lid and cook on High for 20 minutes. Set timer.

4. When timer goes off, turn off pressure cooker and release pressure naturally and add in your broccoli and cook for 5 minutes on High. Set timer. Once timer goes off release pressure and give it a good stir before serving.

5. Serve with your favorite rice or noodles.

Notes

Simple Korean Beef Dinner

COOK TIME
20 MIN
PREP TIME
10 MIN
SERVINGS
6 SERVINGS

INGREDIENTS

- 4 pounds bottom roast, cut into cubes
- Salt and pepper to taste
- 2 tablespoons sesame oil
- 1 cup beef broth
- ½ cup rice wine
- ½ cup soy sauce

- 5 cloves garlic, minced
- 1 medium onion, diced
- 1 tablespoon fresh grated ginger
- ½ cup gochujang
- ¼ cup mirin
- ¼ cup ketchup

PREPARATION

1. Season the cubed roast liberally with salt and pepper. In another mixing bowl whisk together the soy sauce, gochujang, mirin, ketchup and fresh ginger. Coat the meat cubes with this sauce. Set aside.

2. Heat pressure cooker to sauté. Once hot coat add the sesame oil and garlic and onion and sauté for 1 minute. Then add your meat cubes and sauté for another 2-3 minutes. Add in the beef broth and rice wine and give everything a good stir.

3. Once everything is incorporated, lock lid and cook on High for 20 minutes. Set timer. Once timer goes off release pressure naturally.

4. Serve with jasmine rice or udon noodles.

Notes

Spicy Orange Beef

COOK TIME
15 MIN
PREP TIME
10 MIN
SERVINGS
6-8 SERVINGS

INGREDIENTS

- 2 pounds flank steak, cut into 1/4" strips
- 1 tablespoon vegetable oil
- 6 cloves garlic, minced
- ¾ cup fresh orange juice
- ¼ cup soy sauce
- 2 teaspoons sesame oil

- ½ teaspoon red pepper flakes
- 1 teaspoon orange zest
- 2 tablespoon cornstarch
- 3 tablespoon cold water
- 1 bunch green onions, sliced

PREPARATION

1. Season beef with salt and pepper. Put sesame oil in the pressure cooker and brown for 2 minutes - do not crowd. Transfer meat to a plate when browned. When all meat is browned select Sauté and add garlic to the pot. Sauté for 1 minute.

2. Add orange juice, soy sauce, red pepper flakes, and orange zest to the pot. Add browned beef and any accumulated juices. Cook on High for 15 minutes. Set timer.

3. When timer goes off, release pressure naturally. Combine the cornstarch and water, whisking until smooth. Select Simmer and bring to a boil and add cornstarch mixture slowly into the pot stirring constantly, until sauce thickens. Then Stir in the green onions.

4. Serve over rice; garnish with additional orange zest, green onion and red pepper flakes if desired.

Notes

Beefy Beef Patties

COOK TIME
15-20 MIN
PREP TIME
15 MIN
SERVINGS
4 SERVINGS

INGREDIENTS

- 2 pounds ground beef
- 1 egg whisked
- 1 cup ketchup
- 1 can of stew beans
- 1 cup beef stock
- ½ cup diced red peppers and onions
- 2 teaspoon minced garlic

- 1 teaspoon onion powder
- 1 tablespoon Worcestershire
- 1 tablespoons brown sugar
- 1 tablespoons chili powder
- 1 tablespoon yellow mustard
- 1 tablespoon sriracha

PREPARATION

1. In large mixing bowl whisk together the ketchup, onion powder, Worcestershire sauce, brown sugar, chili powder, yellow mustard, sriracha and a crack of fresh pepper and sea salt. Set aside.

2. In another large mixing bowl combine the ground beef with the red peppers and onions and minced garlic and egg. Slowly add the whisked ingredients into the beef until it's well incorporated, but you don't want it to be too wet. Form your patties and place it onto a plate and set aside. (You should be able to form 4 – 6 patties roughly palm sized)

3. Set your pressure cooker to sauté and sauté the stew beans with the beef stock until boiling. Place your patties on top of the bean mixture and lock lid and cook on High for 15 minutes, until its cooked through, set timer. The bean mixture serves as a "jus."

4. Once timer goes off, release pressure naturally and you can serve the patties in a bun with the beans as a "Sloppy Joe" or serve it over jasmine rice or pasta.

Beef Brisket and Honey Carrots

COOK TIME
1 HOUR 10 MIN
PREP TIME
10 MIN
SERVINGS
2-4 SERVINGS

INGREDIENTS

- 2-pound boneless beef brisket, cut into chunks
- 1-2 pounds carrots, peeled and chopped into chunks
- 1 medium red onion cut into thick slices
- 3 tablespoons olive oil
- 1 tablespoon dried mustard powder
- 1 tablespoon paprika

- Salt and pepper to taste
- 1 cup red wine
- 1 cup beef broth
- 2 sprigs of fresh thyme
- ½ cup raw honey

PREPARATION

1. In a mixing bowl, rub the brisket chunks with the mustard powder, paprika and a couple cracks of salt and pepper. Set aside.

2. In another bowl combine the carrots with the raw honey and set aside.

3. In pressure cooker sauté the onions with olive oil for about 1-2 minutes then add in your brisket and brown for about 5 minutes.

4. Add in the honey carrots, then add in the red wine and beef broth and sprigs of fresh thyme. Stir to combine and then lock lid and cook on High for 45 minutes. Set timer.

5. Once timer goes off, release pressure naturally and serve it over rice or pasta.

Notes

Parsley Beef Meatballs

COOK TIME
10-15 MIN
PREP TIME
10 MIN
SERVINGS
4-6 SERVINGS

INGREDIENTS

- 1 medium onion, finely chopped
- 2 cloves minced garlic
- 2 bunches of fresh parsley, finely chopped, discard the stems, only use the leaves
- ¼ teaspoon black pepper

- 2 teaspoons salt
- 1 tablespoon sesame oil
- 1 large egg
- 1 ½ pound ground beef meat
- 1 can beef broth

PREPARATION

1. In a large mixing bowl add the following ingredients to your ground beef:
- 1 medium onion, finely chopped
- 2 cloves minced garlic
- 2 bunches of fresh parsley, finely chopped
- ¼ teaspoon black pepper
- 2 teaspoons salt
- 1 tablespoon sesame oil
- 1 large egg

2. Mix with your hands until everything is incorporated, then crack your egg into the mixture and mix until the egg is incorporated into the meet and seasonings. Set aside the mixture.

3. In your pressure cooker add the can of beef broth, let it heat up on medium and set to 'sauté' mode.

4. Place your meat mixture next to the pressure cooker and start making meatballs – make sure you make them the same size and place each one of the meatballs into your sauce.

5. Keep layering the meatballs into your pressure cooker until you run out of mixture.

6. Close and lock the lid of your pressure cooker and cook for 15 minutes on high. Set timer.

7. Once done cook release pressure naturally and serve with your favorite pasta or jasmine rice. It goes great with a crusty baguette too.

Beef Brisket Risotto

COOK TIME
45 MIN
PREP TIME
10 MIN
SERVINGS
2-4 SERVINGS

INGREDIENTS

- 2 pounds beef brisket cut into small chunks
- 2 cups risotto rice
- 1 cup sliced white mushrooms
- 2 tablespoon smoked sea salt
- 1 teaspoon black pepper
- 1 teaspoon mustard powder

- 1 teaspoon smoked paprika
- 1 tablespoon of olive oil
- 3 cups beef stock
- 2 cups red wine
- 2 fresh thyme sprigs

PREPARATION

1. Place your brisket in a mixing bowl and coat it with the following ingredients:
- 2 tablespoon smoked sea salt
- 1 teaspoon black pepper
- 1 teaspoon mustard powder
- 1 teaspoon smoked paprika

2. Set your pressure cooker to "Sauté" and add olive oil and brown your brisket for about 2 minutes then add in the sliced mushrooms and sauté for another minute.

3. Add in the beef stock and red wine and lock lid and cook on High for 35 minutes. Set timer, once timer goes off release pressure naturally and stir and check the liquid in the pot, if it's not enough, add another cup of beef stock.

4. If the liquid is sufficient then you can add your risotto rice and the fresh sprigs of thyme. Make sure the risotto rice is covered with the liquid. Cook on medium for another 10 minutes. Set timer. Once timer goes off, release pressure naturally. Serve with a side of fresh green salad.

Montreal Dry Rub Short Ribs

COOK TIME
15-20 MIN
PREP TIME
10 MIN
SERVINGS
4-6 SERVINGS

INGREDIENTS

- 3 pounds short ribs
- 1 tablespoon sesame oil
- 4 tablespoons soy sauce
- 2 tablespoons brown sugar

- 1 tablespoon Montreal Steak Seasoning
- 3 Cloves garlic, minced
- 1 teaspoon Tabasco

PREPARATION

1. Combine all the sauce ingredients in a bowl and give it a quick whisk.

2. Heat the oil in the pressure cooker until very hot and add the ribs and sauté for 1 minute, then drizzle the sauce over the ribs. Lock lid and cook on High for 20 minutes. Set timer.

3. Once timer goes off, release pressure naturally and serve with your favorite dipping sauce or a side salad.

Notes

Hearty Vegetable Beef Stew

COOK TIME
30 MIN
PREP TIME
10 MIN
SERVINGS
6 SERVINGS

INGREDIENTS

- 1 pound lean ground beef
- 1 tablespoon olive oil
- 1 large onion, diced
- 1 rib celery, chopped
- 3 cloves garlic, minced
- 2 cans beef broth
- 1 can crushed tomatoes

- 1 bottle Original or Spicy Hot V8 juice
- ½ cup long grain white rice
- 1 can garbanzo beans, drained and rinsed
- 1 large potato, peeled and diced into 1-inch pieces
- 2 carrots, peeled then sliced into thin coins
- ½ cup frozen peas, thawed
- Salt and pepper

PREPARATION

1. Preheat the pressure cooker and sauté ground beef with the oil until browned. Remove to a plate lined with paper towels to soak up excess oil.

2. In pressure cooker, add onion and celery, garlic, beef broth, tomatoes, V8 juice, rice, garbanzo beans, potatoes, and carrots, and bring to a boil, stir to combine. Then add the browned ground and stir to combine. Lock lid and cook on High Pressure for 25 minutes. Set timer.

3. Once timer goes off, release pressure naturally and stir in peas and season with salt and pepper to taste. Add this point you can add more beef stock if you find the stew too thick.

4. Lock lid and cook on High again for another 5 minutes. Set timer. Once timer goes off release pressure and serve with your favorite dinner rolls.

Notes

Baked Potatoes with Beef Bites

COOK TIME
1 HOUR
PREP TIME
15 MIN
SERVINGS
4 SERVINGS

INGREDIENTS

- 4 cups of minced beef, seasoned with 1 tablespoon of dark soy sauce and ½ teaspoon of mustard powder
- 2 large brown rustic potatoes
- Sea salt and pepper
- 1 tablespoon olive oil
- ½ cup onion, finely chopped

PREPARATION

1. Cut your potatoes in half and wrap it in tin foil do not seal it yet. Divide up your seasoned minced beef on top of the potato half along with olive oil, salt and pepper to taste, and a bit of the chopped onion.

2. Repeat process for your other half potatoes.

3. Seal the potatoes in the tin foil.

4. Set your pressure cooker on High, place the potatoes inside, lock lid and set timer for 1 hour. Once timer goes, release pressure naturally and serve with your favorite salad and sour cream.

Notes

Quick and Easy BBQ Meatballs

COOK TIME
20 MIN
PREP TIME
15 MIN
SERVINGS
6 SERVINGS

INGREDIENTS

- 1 bag (48 ounce) frozen fully cooked beef meatballs
- 1 can beef stock
- 1 tablespoon sea salt
- 1 tablespoon white pepper
- 3 cups BBQ Sauce (choose your favorite)
- 3 cups honey

PREPARATION

1. Add beef stock to pressure cooker and add in the beef meatballs, salt and pepper, BBQ sauce and honey.

2. Give it a good stir, lock lid and cook on High for 15 minutes. Set timer.

3. Once timer goes off release pressure and give it another stir. Lock lid and cook on High for another 5 minutes set timer. Once timer goes off, release pressure and serve over your favorite pasta and fresh coriander leaves.

Notes

Chicken

Dinners

Chicken Cuts

Parts

1 – Breast	4 – Wing
2 – Drumstic / Leg	5 – Back
3 – Thig	6 – Neck

Parts

1 – Breast	4 – Wing
2 – Drumstic / Leg	5 – Back
3 – Thig	6 – Neck

Simple Butter Chicken Curry

COOK TIME
20 MIN
PREP TIME
10 MIN
SERVINGS
6-8 SERVINGS

INGREDIENTS

- 8 pieces of small chicken drumsticks
- 4 large tomatoes diced
- 4 small red Thai chili peppers, chopped
- 2 tablespoons fresh ginger, peeled and chopped
- 1 cup of tomato sauce
- ½ cup tomato paste
- ½ cup melted butter
- 2 teaspoons ground cumin

- 1 tablespoon paprika
- 2 teaspoons sea salt
- ½ cup heavy cream
- ¼ cup Greek yogurt
- 2 teaspoons garam masala
- 2 tablespoons cornstarch
- 2 tablespoons water
- ¼ cup firmly packed minced cilantro

PREPARATION

1. Put tomatoes, sauce and paste, Thai peppers and ginger in a blender or food processor and blend to a fine puree.

2. Add butter to pressure cooker and once butter starts to foam add the drumsticks to give them a nice golden brown roughly 10 minutes, season with sea salt and paprika. Once browned, remove and set aside.

3. Add ground cumin to the butter in the pot and cook, stirring quickly. Add the tomato mixtures, salt, cream, yogurt and chicken pieces back into the pot.

4. Gently stir the chicken to coat the pieces. Cover and lock lid, cook on High for 20 minutes, set timer.

5. When timer goes off, release pressure naturally then stir in the garam masala. Whisk together cornstarch and water in a small bowl. Stir the cornstarch mixture slowly into the sauce in the pot, and bring it back to a boil for about 5 minutes.

6. Turn off pressure cooker and stir in minced cilantro. Serve with rice and naan on the side.

Savory Creamy Chicken Breasts

COOK TIME
40 MIN
PREP TIME
10 MIN
SERVINGS
4-6 SERVINGS

INGREDIENTS

- 4 frozen chicken breasts
- 1 cup water
- 2 cups chicken broth
- ½ teaspoon sea salt

- ½ teaspoon dried parsley
- ¼ cup melted butter
- Half a pound of baby carrots
- 1 zucchini, sliced

PREPARATION

1. Place frozen chicken breasts in pressure cooker, add in all the wet ingredients and dry ingredients.

2. Surround the chicken breasts with the baby carrots and sliced zucchini.

3. Cook on medium and set timer for 40 minutes.

4. Once timer goes off, release pressure naturally and check that everything is nice and soft.

5. Serve with rice or Asian noodles with fresh ground pepper. The juices could be turned into a gravy for mash potatoes the next day.

Notes

Spicy Saucy Korean Chicken Drumsticks

COOK TIME
20 MIN
PREP TIME
10 MIN
SERVINGS
6-8 SERVINGS

INGREDIENTS

To make the Korean Sauce
- ½ cup gochujang
- ¼ cup hoisin sauce
- ¼ cup ketchup
- ¼ cup mirin
- ¼ cup soy sauce
- ¼ cup sake rice wine
- 1 tablespoon fresh grated ginger and minced garlic

The Chicken
- 1 tablespoon olive oil
- 1 tablespoon sesame oil
- 8 drumsticks
- 1 chopped medium onion
- 1 cup chicken broth
- 2 teaspoons cornstarch
- ¼ cup water

PREPARATION

1. Whisk all the sauce ingredients together.

2. Set your pressure cooker on High and add the olive oil and sesame oil and quickly brown your drumsticks flipping them over with tongs. Make sure it's brown evenly.

3. Then toss in the onion and let it brown for about a minute. Add the chicken broth to the drumsticks

4. Then add your Korean Sauce to the mixture and give it a good mix.

5. Cover and lock lid in place and cook on High for 20 minutes, set timer.

6. Once timer goes off, release pressure naturally and give it a good stir.

7. You can garnish with fresh parsley or fresh chopped green onion and serve with jasmine rice or over Asian udon.

Orange Zesty Chicken

COOK TIME
10 MIN
PREP TIME
5 MIN
SERVINGS
4-6 SERVINGS

INGREDIENTS

- 4 large boneless skinless chicken breasts diced up
- ¼ cup soy sauce (dark soy preferred)
- ½ cup chicken broth
- 2 tablespoon brown sugar
- 1 tablespoon rice wine
- 1 tablespoon sesame oil
- ¼ teaspoon chili garlic sauce
- ½ cup orange marmalade
- Chili flakes and fresh chopped green onions for garnish

PREPARATION

1. In a bowl whisk together following ingredients:
- ¼ cup soy sauce (dark soy preferred)
- 2 tablespoon brown sugar
- 1 tablespoon rice wine
- ¼ teaspoon chili garlic sauce
- ½ cup orange marmalade

2. Set your pressure cooker on High and add the sesame oil and quickly brown your diced chicken breasts.

3. Add the chicken broth to chicken breasts. Add the whisked ingredients as well.

4. Quickly stir to combine, then cover and lock lid in place and cook on High for 10 minutes. Set timer. Once timer goes off, release pressure and give it a gentle stir.

5. Serve over brown rice and garnish with fresh chopped green onions and chili flakes for an extra kick.

Notes

Shredded Chicken Lettuce Wrap

COOK TIME
35 MIN
PREP TIME
15 MIN
SERVINGS
4 SERVINGS

INGREDIENTS

- 10 medium chicken drumsticks
- 1 can chicken stock
- 1 cup rice wine
- 2 tablespoons white vinegar
- 2 tablespoon sesame oil
- 4 tablespoon dark soy sauce
- 2 tablespoon white pepper

- 2 tablespoon chili flakes
- 3 garlic cloves, minced
- 1 stock of green onion finely chopped
- 1 can of diced pineapples, drained
- 1 head of butter lettuce, peeled with leaves intact and washed, let dry
- Hoisin Sauce for dipping

PREPARATION

1. In large mixing bowl, marinate chicken with soy, sesame oil, pepper, chili flakes and garlic. Set aside.

2. In pressure cooker on High bring to a boil the chicken stock, rice wine, vinegar. Whisk for 2 minutes to incorporate. Then add in the chicken mixture and cook on High for 30 minutes. Lock lid and set timer.

3. Once timer goes off, release pressure naturally and add in the pineapples, lock lid and cook on High for another 5 minutes. Set timer. Once timer goes off release pressure. Use two forks to shred the drumsticks, it does not have to be finely shredded. Stir in the green onion and spoon everything into a serving bowl.

4. To serve, everyone spoons the mixture into their lettuce leaf as if it's a "taco" dip into Hoisin sauce and consume.

Creamy Broccoli Chicken Rice

COOK TIME
15 MIN
PREP TIME
5 MIN
SERVINGS
4 SERVINGS

INGREDIENTS

- 1 tablespoon olive oil
- 1 tablespoon butter
- 2 large boneless, skinless chicken breasts
- ½ cup chopped onion
- 4 cups chicken broth
- ½ teaspoon sea salt
- ½ teaspoon black pepper

- 1/8 teaspoon red pepper flakes
- 1 tablespoon dried parsley
- 2 tablespoons cornstarch
- 2 tablespoons water
- 4 oz. light cream cheese, cut into cubes
- 1 cup shredded cheddar cheese
- 3 cups chopped broccoli

PREPARATION

1. Salt and pepper the chicken breasts. Add oil and butter to pressure cooking pot, and brown the chicken breasts when the butter is sizzling. Remove to a plate and set aside.

2. Add the onion to the pressure cooker, stirring occasionally until its tender. Roughly 5 minutes then stir the chicken broth, salt, pepper, red pepper flakes, and parsley. Mix well, then add the chicken breasts.

3. Set pressure cooker on high for 10 minutes. Set timer. When timer goes off, release pressure naturally and carefully remove the chicken breast to a cutting board and cut into small pieces.

4. Whisk together the cornstarch in 2 tablespoons water in a small bowl. Cook the mixture in the pressure cooker. Once simmered add the cream cheese and shredded cheese. Stir until everything is melted.

5. Add the cutup chicken and broccoli. Cook for another 5 minutes until broccoli and chicken are heated through. Serve with rice and a tossed salad.

Raw Honey Chicken Drumsticks

COOK TIME

40 MIN
PREP TIME
10 MIN
SERVINGS
4 SERVINGS

INGREDIENTS

- 2 pounds Chicken drumsticks
- 1 medium diced Onion
- 2 cloves minced garlic
- ¼ teaspoons Salt
- ¼ teaspoons Black Pepper

- ¼ red pepper flakes
- 1 cup honey
- 1 cup soy sauce
- 1 cup chicken stock
- 2 tablespoons olive oil

PREPARATION

1. In mixing bowl mix together the following ingredients:
- 2 pounds Chicken drumsticks
- 1 medium diced Onion
- 2 cloves minced garlic
- ¼ teaspoons Salt
- ¼ teaspoons Black Pepper
- ¼ red pepper flakes
- 1 cup honey
- 1 cup soy sauce

2. In your pressure cooker set to Medium and heat up the chicken stock with the olive oil. Once the stock is boiling place your chicken mixture into pressure cooker.

3. Set timer for 40 minutes. Once timer goes off release pressure naturally. Serve over rice or pasta.

Notes

Soy Butter Chicken

COOK TIME
15 MIN
PREP TIME
10 MIN
SERVINGS
4-6 SERVINGS

INGREDIENTS

- 8 medium size drumsticks
- 1 large onion chopped
- 1 large carrot chopped
- 1 cup soy sauce (dark soy preferred)
- 1 cup chicken broth
- 1 cup water
- ½ cup of melted butter (this is what makes it buttery and moist)

- ¼ cup Honey
- 1 tablespoon rice wine
- 1 tablespoon sesame oil
- 1 tablespoon olive oil
- 1 tablespoon minced fresh garlic
- 1 tablespoon Chili flakes

PREPARATION

1. In a bowl whisk together following ingredients:
- 1 cup soy sauce (dark soy preferred)
- 1 cup chicken broth
- 1 cup water
- ½ cup of melted butter (this is what makes it buttery and moist)
- ¼ cup Honey
- 1 tablespoon rice wine
- 1 tablespoon sesame oil
- 1 tablespoon olive oil
- 1 tablespoon minced fresh garlic
- 1 tablespoon Chili flakes

2. Set your pressure cooker on medium, once it's hot add sesame and olive oil and quickly brown your drumsticks.

3. Once drumsticks are browned place your carrots and onion over the drumsticks and pour in your whisked mixture.

4. Cover and Lock lid and cook on High. Set timer for 15 minutes. Once timer goes off, release pressure and give it a gentle stir.

5. Serve over brown rice or udon and garnish with fresh parsley.

Easy Chicken Pot Pie Stew

COOK TIME
45 MIN
PREP TIME
5 MIN
SERVINGS
6-8 SERVINGS

INGREDIENTS

- 4 large frozen chicken breasts
- 1 large onion, chopped
- 2 cups frozen mixed vegetables
- Salt and pepper

- 5 cups of chicken broth
- 1 cup heavy cream (or milk)
- 2 tablespoon flour

PREPARATION

1. Put your frozen chicken breasts, chopped onion, salt and pepper and 4 cups of the chicken broth into your pressure cooker.

2. Lock the lid and set it to "Soup/Stew" setting and set timer for 40 minutes.

3. Once timer goes off carefully release pressure naturally and remove lid. Take out the chicken breasts and place on cutting board let it cool before cutting into small pieces, and add it back into the pot.

4. Cook on high and let the broth boil again and then add the frozen vegetables to the broth, stir well.

5. Mix in the 1 cup of heavy cream with the flour and pour into the soup to thicken. Adjust seasoning to your liking, then lock lid and cook on High for another 5 minutes. Set timer and once timer goes off release pressure naturally and serve with warm bread or dinner rolls.

Notes

Chicken Parmesan Meatballs

COOK TIME
30 MIN
PREP TIME
15 MIN
SERVINGS
4 SERVINGS

PLEASE NOTE: THE INGREDIENTS ARE BEST MADE THE DAY BEFORE, TO ALLOW FOR THE MEATBALLS TO MARINATE.

INGREDIENTS

- 1 pound ground chicken
- ½ cup seasoned breadcrumbs
- 1 cup freshly grated Parmesan cheese
- 2 shallots, minced
- 1 garlic clove, minced
- Small handful of chopped parsley
- ¼ teaspoon salt
- ¼ teaspoon pepper
- 1 egg, beaten
- 1 tablespoon olive oil
- 1 can chicken broth
- 2 teaspoons ranch dressing
- 2 ounces cream cheese
- 1 teaspoon lemon juice

PREPARATION

1. In large mixing bowl combine the following:
- 1 pound ground chicken
- ½ cup seasoned breadcrumbs
- 1 cup freshly grated Parmesan cheese
- 2 shallots, minced
- 1 garlic clove, minced
- Small handful of chopped parsley
- ¼ teaspoon salt
- ¼ teaspoon pepper
- 1 egg, beaten
- 1 tablespoon olive oil

2. Once combined, start rolling the chicken mixture into golf ball sized meatballs and lay them out on a tray. Refrigerate for at least 30 minutes or overnight. Once ready to cook, brown your meat balls in a skillet with olive oil until it's a nice golden color. Set pressure cooker on High and combine chicken broth, ranch dressing, cream cheese and lemon juice.

3. Place a layer of the meatballs into pressure cooker. Do not over crowd. Lock lid and cook on High for 30 minutes. Set timer. Once timer goes off, release pressure naturally and sever the meatballs over your favorite pasta and a fresh garden salad.

Kung-Po Chili Chicken

COOK TIME
25 MIN
PREP TIME
30 MIN
SERVINGS
4-6 SERVINGS

PLEASE NOTE: FOR BEST RESULTS MARINATE THE CHICKEN THE NIGHT BEFORE.

INGREDIENTS

- 2 tablespoon olive oil for sauté
- 350 grams boneless chicken, diced
- 1 egg, slightly beaten
- ½ cup corn flour
- 1 tablespoon soy sauce
- 2 tablespoon vinegar
- ½ teaspoon garlic paste

- ½ teaspoon ginger paste
- 1 tablespoon salt
- 2 cups onions, thickly sliced
- 1 cup sliced white mushrooms
- 1 red bell pepper, diced
- 2 green chilies, thickly sliced (remove seeds if too hot)

PREPARATION

1. Mix together the chicken, egg, corn-flour, ginger and garlic paste, 2 teaspoon salt, and enough water so that the chicken pieces are coated with the batter. Leave this for about 30 minutes to marinate (best if this was done the night before)

2. Set pressure cook on High and sauté the chicken and onion with olive oil until onion is tender 5 minutes.

Then add in the red bell pepper, green chilies, mushrooms, soy sauce and vinegar. Give it a good stir then lock lid and cook on High for 20 minutes. Set timer.

3. Once timer goes off, release pressure and serve with rice and lime wedges.

Notes

Sticky Sriracha Honey Wings

COOK TIME
30 MIN
PREP TIME
15 MIN
SERVINGS
4-6 SERVINGS

INGREDIENTS

- 3 pounds chicken wings
- Salt and pepper (used to season wings)
- 1 tablespoon sesame oil
- 3 tablespoons melted butter
- 1 cup Sriracha Sauce

- 1 cup honey
- 1 tablespoon rice wine
- 1 teaspoon soy sauce
- 1 teaspoon hoisin sauce
- 2 tablespoons chopped cilantro

PREPARATION

1. In a large bowl, toss the wings generously with salt and pepper and sesame oil. Then add the butter, Sriracha, honey, soy sauce, rice wine, and hoisin sauce. Coat evenly then set aside.

2. Set pressure cooker on High and add in the wings mixture. Lock lid and cook for 30 minutes. Set timer.

3. Once timer goes off, release pressure naturally and remove from pressure cooker. Sprinkle the cilantro and serve with fresh celery sticks.

Notes

Lemon Butter Wings

COOK TIME
30 MIN
PREP TIME
15 MIN
SERVINGS
4-6 SERVINGS

INGREDIENTS

- 3 pounds chicken wings
- Salt and pepper (used to season wings)
- 1 tablespoon sesame oil

- 1 stick of butter
- 2 tablespoon soy sauce
- Juice of one lemon

PREPARATION

1. In a large bowl, toss the wings generously with salt and pepper and sesame oil and soy sauce.

2. Set pressure cooker on High and add in the wings mixture, butter, and lemon juice. Lock lid and cook for 30 minutes. Set timer.

3. Once timer goes off, release pressure naturally and remove from pressure cooker. Serve with your favorite dinner rolls.

Notes

Spicy BBQ Saucy Wings

COOK TIME
30 MIN
PREP TIME
15 MIN
SERVINGS
4-6 SERVINGS

INGREDIENTS

- 3 pounds chicken wings
- Salt and pepper (used to season wings)
- 3 tablespoon sesame oil
- ½ cup tomato paste

- 4 tablespoons soy sauce
- 4 tablespoons white vinegar
- 1 cup red wine
- ½ cup chili hot sauce

PREPARATION

1. In a large bowl, toss the wings generously with salt and pepper and sesame oil and soy sauce.

2. Set pressure cooker on High and add in the wings mixture, then add in the rest of the wet ingredients and cook for 30 minutes. Set timer.

3. Once timer goes off, release pressure naturally and remove from pressure cooker. Serve with your favorite cucumber slices and celery sticks.

Notes

Spicy Thai Chicken Wings

COOK TIME
30 MIN
PREP TIME
15 MIN
SERVINGS
4-6 SERVINGS

INGREDIENTS

- 20 chicken wings, arm of the wing intact
- 4 cloves minced garlic
- 1 tablespoon cracked black pepper
- 1 tablespoon palm sugar, grated

- 1 tablespoon soy sauce
- 2 tablespoon sesame oil
- 2 tablespoon lime juice
- 1 tablespoon chili garlic sauce to taste

PREPARATION

1. In a large bowl, toss the wings generously with salt and pepper and sesame oil and soy sauce.

2. Set pressure cooker on High and add in the wings mixture, then add in the rest of the wet ingredients and cook for 30 minutes. Set timer.

3. Once timer goes off, release pressure naturally and remove from pressure cooker. Serve with your favorite cucumber slices and celery sticks.

Notes

Balsamic Style Chicken Wings

COOK TIME
30 MIN
PREP TIME
15 MIN
SERVINGS
4-6 SERVINGS

INGREDIENTS

- 20 chicken wings, arm of the wing intact
- 4 cloves minced garlic
- 1 tablespoon cracked black pepper
- 1 tablespoon soy sauce

- 2 tablespoon sesame oil
- ½ cup lime juice
- 1 cup honey
- 1 cup balsamic vinegar

PREPARATION

1. In a large bowl, toss the wings generously with salt and pepper and sesame oil and soy sauce.

2. Set pressure cooker on High and add in the wings mixture, then add in the rest of the wet ingredients and cook for 30 minutes. Set timer.

3. Once timer goes off, release pressure and remove from pressure naturally cooker. Serve with your favorite cucumber slices and celery sticks.

Notes

Coconut Chili Chicken Wings

COOK TIME
30 MIN
PREP TIME
15 MIN
SERVINGS
4-6 SERVINGS

INGREDIENTS

- 20 chicken wings, arm of the wing intact
- Salt and pepper
- 4 cloves minced garlic
- 1 can chicken stock

- 1 can coconut milk
- 4 Thai small chilies, diced
- 1 tablespoon soy sauce
- 2 tablespoon sesame oil

PREPARATION

1. In a large bowl, toss the wings generously with salt and pepper and sesame oil.

2. Set pressure cooker on High and add in the wings mixture, then add in the rest of the wet ingredients and cook for 30 minutes. Set timer.

3. Once timer goes off, release pressure naturally and remove from pressure cooker. Serve with your favorite cucumber slices and celery sticks.

Notes

Honey Sesame Chicken

COOK TIME
20 MIN
PREP TIME
15 MIN
SERVINGS
6 SERVINGS

INGREDIENTS

- 4 large boneless skinless chicken breasts, diced
- Salt and pepper
- 1 tablespoon olive oil
- ½ cup diced onion
- 2 cloves garlic, minced
- ½ cup soy sauce
- ¼ cup ketchup

- 2 teaspoons sesame oil
- 1 cup honey
- 2 tablespoon toasted sesame seeds
- ¼ teaspoon red pepper flakes
- 2 tablespoons cornstarch
- 3 tablespoons water
- 2 green onions, thinly sliced

PREPARATION

1. Season the chicken with salt and pepper. Preheat pressure cooker. Add oil and sauté onion, garlic, and chicken to the pot and sauté stirring occasionally until onion is softened, about 3 minutes. Add soy sauce, ketchup, and red pepper flakes to the pressure cooking pot and stir to combine.

2. Pressure cook on high for 20 minutes. Set timer. When timer goes off, release pressure naturally. Add sesame oil and honey to the pot and stir to combine. In a small bowl, dissolve cornstarch in water and add to the pot stirring slowly. Select Sauté and simmer until sauce thickens. Stir in green onions and toasted sesame seed for another 2 minutes. Serve over rice or pasta.

Notes

Chicken and Corn Meatballs

COOK TIME
15 MIN
PREP TIME
10 MIN
SERVINGS
4-6 SERVINGS

INGREDIENTS

- 1 medium onion, finely chopped
- 1 cup corn tidbits
- 2 cloves minced garlic
- ½ teaspoon dried oregano
- ½ teaspoon dried parsley
- ¼ teaspoon black pepper

- 2 teaspoons salt
- 1 tablespoon olive oil
- 1 large egg
- 2 pound ground chicken meat
- 2 cups chicken stock

PREPARATION

1. In a large mixing bowl add the following ingredients to your ground chicken:
- 1 medium onion, finely chopped
- 1 cup corn tidbits
- 2 cloves minced garlic
- ½ teaspoon dried oregano
- ½ teaspoon dried parsley
- ¼ teaspoon black pepper
- 2 teaspoons salt
- 1 tablespoon olive oil

2. Mix with your hands until everything is incorporated, then crack your egg into the mixture and mix until the egg is incorporated into the meat and seasonings. Set aside the mixture. In your pressure cooker add the chicken stock and let it heat up on medium and set to 'sauté' mode.

3. Place your meat mixture next to the pressure cooker and start making meatballs – make sure you make them the same size and place each one of the meatballs into liquid. Do not over crowd.

4. Close and lock the lid of your pressure cooker and cook for 15 minutes on high. Set timer.

5. Once done cooking release pressure naturally and serve with your favorite pasta or jasmine rice.

Butternut Squash Soup with Chicken Orzo

COOK TIME
25 MIN
PREP TIME
15 MIN
SERVINGS
6 SERVINGS

INGREDIENTS

- 1 ½ pounds of fresh baked butternut squash (peeled, and cubed)
- 3 tablespoons melted butter
- ½ cup green onions, diced
- ½ cup celery, diced
- ½ cup carrots, diced
- 1 garlic clove, minced
- 4 cups chicken broth
- 1 can diced tomatoes with juice

- ½ teaspoon Italian seasoning
- 1/8 teaspoon dried red pepper flakes
- ¼ teaspoon freshly ground black pepper
- 1/8 teaspoon freshly grated nutmeg
- 1 cup orzo, cooked
- 1 cup chicken breasts, cooked and diced seasoned with salt and pepper to taste
- ½ to 1 cup half and half cream
- Green onions, sliced very thin for garnish

PREPARATION

1. Melt butter in pressure cooker pot. Sauté onions, celery, and carrots. Add garlic, stir briefly and add chicken stock, tomatoes and squash. Add Italian seasoning, red pepper flakes, pepper and nutmeg.

2. Lock lid and cook on High for 20 minutes. Set timer. Once timer goes off, release pressure naturally.

3. Spoon the cooked vegetables into a blender along with any liquid and puree until mixture is very smooth. Set aside.

4. Add the cooked chicken and orzo and cream. Bring to a boil, then add the blended butternut squash mixture back into the pressure cooker. Lock lid and cook on High for 5 minutes. Set timer. Once timer goes off, release pressure naturally and give everything inside the pressure cooker a good stir. Add salt and pepper to taste serve with dinner rolls and garnish with sliced green onions.

Pork
Dinners

Pork Cuts

Parts

1 - Head	6 - Loin	11 - Arm shoulder
2 - Ear	7 - Rump	12 - Hocks
3 - Jowl	8 - Leg / Ham	13 - Feets / Trotters
4 - Shoulder	9 - Belly / Bacon	14 - Tale
5 - Rack	10 - Spare Ribs	

Parts

1 - Head	6 - Loin	11 - Arm shoulder
2 - Ear	7 - Rump	12 - Hocks
3 - Jowl	8 - Leg / Ham	13 - Feets / Trotters
4 - Shoulder	9 - Belly / Bacon	14 - Tale
5 - Rack	10 - Spare Ribs	

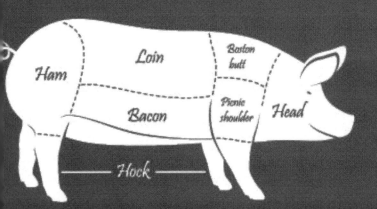

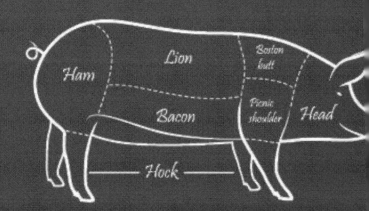

Family Style Pork Roast

COOK TIME
60 MIN
PREP TIME
15 MIN
SERVINGS
4-6 SERVINGS

INGREDIENTS

- 1 (3 pound) pork roast
- 12 oz. vegetable stock
- 1 teaspoon of sea salt and pepper
- ¼ teaspoon rosemary
- ¼ teaspoon oregano
- ¼ teaspoon dried parsley flakes

- ½ teaspoon onion flakes
- ¼ teaspoon paprika
- 2 tablespoon olive oil
- 1 pound baby carrots
- 1 onion roughly chopped
- 2 large russet potatoes peeled and cut into chunks

PREPARATION

1. In a glass bowl mix together your seasoning to create a rub. Whisk together the olive oil with rosemary, oregano, parsley flakes, onion flakes, and paprika. Rub it thoroughly on your pork roast.

2. Rinse and pat pork roast dry season it. On sauté mode, add oil in the pressure cooker and once its sizzling brown the pork roast. Brown each side evenly for about 5 minutes, or until golden brown. Leave it in the pressure cooker.

3. Add 12 vegetable stock to pressure cooker and surround the pork roast with carrots, onions and potatoes and cook on Medium for 60 minutes. Set timer.

4. Once timer goes off, release pressure naturally and open lid and transfer the pork roast to a carving dish and transfer the vegetables into another serving bowl. Serve with rice or a green salad.

Notes

Honey Dijon Mustard Pork Chops

COOK TIME
15 MIN
PREP TIME
10 MIN
SERVINGS
4 SERVINGS

INGREDIENTS

- 4 medium size pork chops
- 3 cloves garlic, roughly chopped
- 1 small onion, sliced
- 1 tablespoon olive oil
- ½ cup chicken stock
- ¼ cup honey

- 1 tablespoon Worcestershire sauce
- 1 tablespoon Dijon mustard
- 1 teaspoon paprika
- 1 ½ tablespoon cornstarch + 2 tablespoons water
- Salt & black pepper to taste

PREPARATION

1. Tenderize the pork chops with a small meat hammer. Then generously season the pork chops with black pepper and salt.

2. Set your pressure cooker on High and roughly brown pork chops and set aside.

3. Then sauté the onions with garlic in pressure cooker.

4. Pour in chicken stock and add honey and Worcestershire sauce, Dijon mustard, and paprika. Stir well.

5. Place browned pork chops back into the pressure cooker. Close and lock lid. Cook on High and set timer for 15 minutes. Once timer goes off release pressure naturally.

6. Serve with jasmine rice, pasta or dinner rolls.

Notes

Italian Sausages and Peppers

COOK TIME
30 MIN
PREP TIME
15 MIN
SERVINGS
6 SERVINGS

INGREDIENTS

- 10 Italian spice sausages
- 2 large green bell peppers, seeded cored and cut into thin strips
- 2 large yellow bell peppers, seeded cored and cut into thin strips
- 4 tomatoes diced
- 2 gloves garlic, minced
- 1 can of your favorite tomato sauce
- 1 cup beef stock
- 1 tablespoon dried parsley flakes
- 1 tablespoon dried oregano

PREPARATION

1. In the pressure cooker combine the following ingredients and stir well:
- 4 tomatoes diced
- 2 gloves garlic, minced
- 1 can of your favorite tomato sauce
- 1 cup beef stock
- 1 tablespoon dried parsley flakes
- 1 tablespoon dried oregano

2. Layer the sausages on top of the sauce in pressure cooker, then layer the peppers on top of the sausages. Do not stir.

3. Lock lid in place and cook on High for 30 minutes. Set timer. Once timer goes off release pressure naturally.

4. Season with fresh crack of pepper and serve with a side of jasmine rice or warm dinner rolls.

Notes

Traditional Pork and Beans

COOK TIME
40 MIN
PREP TIME
15 MIN
SERVINGS
6 SERVINGS

INGREDIENTS

- 1 pound dried navy beans
- 8 cups chicken stock
- 1 tablespoon salt
- 8 slices thick-sliced bacon, cut into ½ inch pieces
- 1 large green bell pepper cut into thin slices
- 2 tablespoon sesame oil
- 1 large onion, chopped

- 2 ½ cups water
- ½ cup ketchup
- ¼ cup packed brown sugar
- 1 teaspoon dry mustard powder
- ½ teaspoon salt
- ¼ teaspoon ground black pepper

PREPARATION

1. Rinse beans in cold water to remove any debris with a colander. Soak beans for 10 minutes, while you prepare the other ingredients.

2. In mixing bowl mix together bacon and peppers with ketchup, brown sugar, mustard powder, salt and pepper.

3. In your pressure cooker, sauté the onion on high for 5 minutes, then add the chicken stock and water. Drain your beans and add the beans into the pot too. Cook on High for 30 minutes. Lock lid and set timer.

4. Once timer goes off, release pressure, and add in your pork mixture, with another cup of chicken stock. Give it a good stir. Lock lid and cook on High for another 10 minutes. Set timer. Once timer goes off release pressure naturally and serve with your warm dinner rolls and a garden salad.

Raw Honey Orange Pork

COOK TIME
40 MIN
PREP TIME
15 MIN
SERVINGS
6 SERVINGS

INGREDIENTS

- 1 pound pork shoulder meat, sliced
- 1 juice of an orange
- 1 cinnamon stick
- 3 garlic cloves, minced
- 1 small onion, sliced
- 1 tablespoon ginger, sliced
- 2 cloves garlic, minced

- A pinch of dried rosemary
- 1 cup chicken stock
- 2 tablespoons light soy sauce
- ½ cup raw honey
- 1 tablespoon olive oil
- Kosher salt and black pepper

PREPARATION

1. Season the pork with generous amount of kosher salt and ground black pepper.

2. Heat up your pressure cooker. Add 1 tablespoon of olive oil and pork shoulder to the pressure cooker, then brown it for 3 to 5 minutes on each side. Remove and set aside.

3. Reduce the heat to medium. Add the sliced onions, ginger, a pinch of kosher salt and ground black pepper. Cook the onions and ginger for 1 minute. Add garlic and stir for 30 seconds. Then add your pork and the rest of the ingredients into the pot. Lock lid and cook on High for 30 minutes. Set timer. Once timer goes off release pressure naturally and check on the juices of the pork. If it's too thin add 1 cup of water and pinch of kosher salt. Lock lid and cook on High for another 10 minutes. Set timer. Once timer goes off release pressure and serve over rice or pasta.

4. To thicken the sauce for a gravy: Mix the cornstarch with water, then mix it into the sauce one-third at a time until desired thickness. Turn off pressure cooker and place the pork in the sauce and coat it evenly.

Mushroom Onion Gravy Pork Chops

COOK TIME
20 MIN
PREP TIME
5 MIN
SERVINGS
4-6 SERVINGS

INGREDIENTS

- 4 bone-in thick pork chops
- 2 tablespoons olive oil
- 1 ½ cups water

- 1 can condensed cream of mushroom soup
- 1 large mushroom, sliced
- ½ tablespoon Lemon pepper

PREPARATION

1. Rinse and pat pork chops dry and season liberally with Lemon Pepper (or your favorite seasoning).

2. Brown oil in pressure cooker, then quickly brown pork chops on both sides in the pot. When browned set aside the pork chops.

3. Add water to deglaze the pot and stir in the mushroom soup, and onions then add the pork chops back into the pressure cooker.

4. Lock lid in place and cook on High. Set timer for 20 minutes. When timer goes off release pressure naturally and carefully remove lid.

5. Serve each pork chop on individual plates with pasta or rice and pour the mushroom gravy over the pork chops.

Notes

Pork Sirloin Tip Roast

COOK TIME
35 MIN
PREP TIME
15 MIN
SERVINGS
6 SERVINGS

INGREDIENTS

- 3 pound pork sirloin tip roast
- ½ teaspoon coarse black pepper
- ½ teaspoon salt
- ½ teaspoon onion powder
- ½ teaspoon garlic powder

- ¼ teaspoon chili powder
- 1 tablespoon vegetable oil
- 1 cup chicken stock
- ½ cup apple juice

PREPARATION

1. Mix together spices in a small bowl and rub spice mixture all over pork roast. Put oil in the cooking pot and brown on both sides.

2. Add the chicken stock and apple juice to the pressure cooker.

3. Lock lid in place and cook on High for 35 minutes and set timer. Once timer goes off release pressure naturally and serve with your favorite sides and dinner rolls.

Notes

Pork Stroganoff

COOK TIME
25-30 MIN
PREP TIME
15 MIN
SERVINGS
6 SERVINGS

INGREDIENTS

- 2 pound pork sirloin tip roast, diced
- 3 tablespoons olive oil, divided
- 1 large onion, finely chopped
- ¼ cup dry sherry
- 2 tablespoons chili sauce
- 1 teaspoon dry mustard

- 1 can chicken broth
- 1 tablespoon butter
- ½ pound fresh mushrooms, sliced
- 2 tablespoons cornstarch
- 3 tablespoons cold water
- ½ cup sour cream
- Salt & pepper

PREPARATION

1. Season pork generously with salt and pepper. Put 1 tablespoon oil in the pressure cooker and brown - do not crowd, add more oil as needed. Transfer meat to a plate when browned.

2. Sauté onions and cook, stirring frequently, until the onions soften and begin to brown, about 3 minutes. Then add in your pork and the rest of the ingredients, not including the cornstarch, water or sour cream. Give it a good stir then lock lid and cook on High for 20 minutes. Set timer. Once timer goes off release pressure and give it a good stir. Season to taste and lock lid and cook again for another 10 minutes on High. Set timer. Once timer goes off release pressure naturally and scoop pork into serving dish.

3. Combine the cornstarch and water, whisking until smooth. Add cornstarch mixture to the broth in the pot stirring constantly. Select Simmer and bring to a boil, stirring constantly until sauce thickens. Add 1/3 cup of gravy to the sour cream and mix until well combined.

4. Add the sour cream mixture to the gravy and stir until well blended. Stir in the pork again and serve over jasmine rice or pasta.

Greek Tacos

COOK TIME
20 MIN
PREP TIME
15 MIN
SERVINGS
6 SERVINGS

INGREDIENTS

- 2 tablespoon olive oil
- 1 cup diced red onion
- 4 cloves garlic, minced
- 1 pound ground pork
- 1 tablespoon Oregano
- 1 ½ tsp black pepper

- 1 tablespoon kosher salt
- ½ cup sun dried tomatoes
- 1 cup cherry tomatoes, quartered
- 1 cup cucumber, diced
- 1 tablespoon lemon juice
- 2 tablespoon red wine vinegar

PREPARATION

1. In your pressure cooker sauté on High the onions in the olive oil for about 5 minutes, add the garlic, sauté 1 minute, then add the ground pork and sauté until golden brown for about 5.

2. Add the oregano, black pepper, kosher salt and sun dried tomatoes and cucumbers, lemon juice and red wine vinegar to the pork mixture stir to combine everything.

3. Lock lid and cook on High for 15 minutes. Set timer. Once timer goes off, release pressure naturally and serve in hard shell tacos with guacamole and sour cream.

Notes

Easy Pulled Pork and Beans Taco Dinner

COOK TIME
45 MIN
PREP TIME
10 MIN
SERVINGS
4-6 SERVINGS

INGREDIENTS

- 2 tablespoons olive oil
- 4 pounds. boneless pork shoulder, cut into 4 pieces
- 1 can cooked pork beans (choose your favorite kind)
- 2 cups barbecue sauce

- ½ teaspoon black pepper
- ½ teaspoon sea salt
- Pinch of paprika
- Pinch of oregano
- Pinch of Cayenne pepper
- ½ cup water

PREPARATION

1. Brown the pork pieces on both sides with the oil in pressure cooker 2-3 minutes per side. Once browned, set aside.

2. Mix 2 cup barbecue sauce and ½ cup water into the pressure cooker. Stir to combine and add the beans then the pork back into the pressure cooker and the rest of the seasoning.

3. Cook on High and set the timer for 45 minutes. When timer goes off release pressure naturally.

4. Remove the pork from the pressure cooker and shred with two forks.

5. Put the shredded pork back into pressure cooker and bring it back to a simmer and mix well.

6. Serve on warm taco shells with your favorite toppings or on toasted rolls.

Notes

Hamburger Pork Patties in Jus

COOK TIME
10 MIN
PREP TIME
15 MIN
SERVINGS
4 SERVINGS

INGREDIENTS

- 2 pounds of ground pork
- ½ cup bread crumbs
- 2 eggs, beaten
- 3 cloves garlic, minced
- 1 small onion, minced
- 1 tablespoon sesame oil
- 1 tablespoon dried parsley flakes
- 1 tablespoon salt and pepper, mixed
- 1 tablespoon soy sauce

- 1 tablespoon Worcestershire sauce
- 1 tablespoon Dijon mustard

FOR THE JUS
- 2 cans beef stock
- ½ cup rice wine
- 1 sprig of rosemary
- 1 sprig of thyme

PREPARATION

1. In large mixing bowl combine all the above ingredients and mix well.

2. Start forming your patties. You want them at least 1 inch thick and palm size, gently flattened. This should yield 4-5 patties (you can determine the thickness and size, but if it's too thin it will fall apart when cooking in the Jus)

3. Once patties are formed, heat up a frying pan with olive oil and grill each side of the patters for 3 minutes or until golden brown.

4. Set your pressure cooker on High and add the ingredients for the Jus. Bring to a boil and place 4 patties at a time do not over crowd. Lock lid and cook for 10 minutes. Set timer.

5. Once timer goes off, release pressure naturally and gently scoop out your patties and serve on your favorite bun with fresh romaine lettuce and sliced tomatoes.

6. For the remaining Jus you can save it and turn it into a gravy for your next meal.

Chilies

Curries

Green Chili Chicken Curry

COOK TIME
15 MIN
PREP TIME
10 MIN
SERVINGS
4-6 SERVINGS

INGREDIENTS

- 3 pounds bone-in skin-on chicken thighs and drumsticks
- 4 tomatillos, quartered, husks discarded
- 3 poblano peppers, roughly chopped, seeds and stems discarded
- 2 Anaheim peppers, roughly chopped, seeds and stems discarded
- 2 jalapeño chilies, roughly chopped, stems discarded

- 1 medium white onion, roughly chopped
- 6 cloves garlic, peeled
- 1 tablespoon whole cumin seed, toasted and ground
- Sea salt
- ½ cup loosely packed fresh cilantro leaves
- 1 tablespoon Asian fish
- Lime and fresh jalapeño peppers for garnish

PREPARATION

1. Combine chicken, tomatillos, and all the peppers, garlic, onion, cumin, and a big pinch of salt in pressure cooker. Cook on High for 15 minutes. Set timer.

2. Once timer goes off, release pressure and carefully open lid and transfer chicken pieces to a bowl and set aside.

3. Add cilantro and fish sauce to the pressure cooker and mix with a whisk and season with some salt and pepper to taste.

4. Add the chicken back into the sauce and stir well. Once all mixed, transfer everything from the pressure cooker to a serving bowl.

5. Serve immediately with tortillas and lime wedges.

Chili Dog Sauce

COOK TIME
40 MIN
PREP TIME
15 MIN
SERVINGS
4-6 SERVINGS

INGREDIENTS

- 1 can of Mexican pinto beans
- 1 cup beef stock
- ½ pound ground beef
- ¼ cup tomato paste
- 2 tablespoon Dijon

- 1 onion minced
- 2 tablespoon chili oil
- 2 tablespoon chili powder
- 2 tablespoon Worcestershire sauce
- 1 tablespoon salt and 2 cracks of fresh pepper

PREPARATION

1. In large mixing bowl combine the following and set aside:
- ½ pound ground beef
- ¼ cup tomato paste
- 2 tablespoon Dijon
- 1 onion minced
- 2 tablespoon chili oil
- 2 tablespoon chili powder
- 2 tablespoon Worcestershire sauce
- 1 tablespoon salt and 2 cracks of fresh pepper

2. Set pressure cooker on High and add the beans and beef stock, bring to boil and use large wooden spoon to stir and mash up the beans for 5 minutes.

3. Add in the beef mixture and lock lid and cook on high for 40 minutes. Set timer.

4. Once timer goes off release pressure. Give it a good stir and adjust seasoning to taste, you can add a few drops of tabasco if desired. Serve over hot dogs and a sprinkle of cheddar.

Jumbo Shrimp Curry

COOK TIME
10 MIN
PREP TIME
8-10 MIN
SERVINGS
4 SERVINGS

INGREDIENTS

- 1 pound frozen jumbo shrimp, thawed and peeled
- Salt and White Pepper
- 1 tablespoon dried parsley
- 1 tablespoon Sesame oil
- 1 tablespoon rice wine
- 1 small onion, diced
- 1 green pepper, diced
- 1 tablespoon olive oil

FOR THOSE WHO DECIDE TO MAKE THEIR OWN YELLOW CURRY PASTE

Replace the simplified version with 1 cup of Curry Paste and half a can of coconut milk and half a can of chicken broth.

For the Curry (simplified version)

- ½ tablespoon grated fresh ginger
- 1 diced red Thai chili pepper
- 2 cloves minced garlic
- 1 can of chicken broth
- 1 can of coconut milk
- 1 cup of yellow curry powder (choose your favorite)
- 1 tablespoon cornstarch + cold water (this is used to thicken the curry only if it's not thick enough)

PREPARATION

1. In a large mixing bowl marinate your shrimp with the following ingredients then set aside:

   - Salt and White Pepper
   - 1 tablespoon dried parsley
   - 1 tablespoon Sesame oil
   - 1 tablespoon rice wine

2. In another bowl whisk together the chicken broth and coconut milk then slowly add the curry powder. Whisk well. Then add the minced garlic, Thai chili pepper and ginger. Set aside.

3. Turn pressure cooker on high and sauté the onion and green pepper with olive oil, once onion is tender. Add the curry mixture and add the marinated shrimp.

Cover and lock lid and cook on High for 8 minutes. Set timer.

4. Once timer goes off. Release pressure and give the curry a good stir. If it is not at your desired thickness, add the cornstarch mixture in small amounts and mix well.

How to make your own
Curry Paste

For those of you who want to make your own **Curry Paste from scratch**. This recipe does take about 45 minutes and it's something that you need to make ahead of time. Once you have made your own Yellow Curry Paste, you can cook with this instead of cooking with the simplified version. Replace the simplified version with 1 cup of Yellow Curry Paste and half a can of coconut milk and half a can of chicken broth.

PREPARATION

1. Preheat the oven to 350 degrees. Lay out a large piece of tin foil onto a baking sheet and lay out the following ingredients:
- 5 large shallots, peeled
- 5 large heads of garlic, clove, peeled and ends cut off
- Drizzle oil over the garlic and shallots. Wrap them up and seal the tin foil, and let it bake for 35 minutes.

2. While it's baking soak the chilies in warm water for 15 minutes. Drain and set aside. Once the garlic and shallots are done baking put it in a food processor along with the chilies and the following ingredients:

5. Season with salt and pepper to taste. Serve over jasmine rice or Asian egg noodles. It's great for dipping crusty baguettes too!

*For a spicier version dice up 5-10 red Thai chili peppers and add it to the curry mixture before cooking.

INGREDIENTS

- 5 large shallots, peeled
- 5 large heads of garlic, clove, peeled and ends cut off
- 10 whole dried Thai chili peppers
- 1½ tablespoons salt
- 3 tablespoons turmeric
- 3 tablespoons mild yellow curry powder
- 3 teaspoons ground coriander
- ½ cup packed cilantro leaves and stems
- 1 small piece of ginger grated about ¼ cup of fresh ginger

- 1½ tablespoons salt
- 3 tablespoons turmeric
- 3 tablespoons mild yellow curry powder
- 3 teaspoons roasted ground coriander
- ½ cup packed cilantro leaves and stems
- 1 small piece of ginger grated about ¼ cup of fresh ginger

3. Pulse or puree until the yellow curry paste reaches your desired consistency. The recipe should make about 2 cups of curry paste. The paste keeps for about a week in the fridge and it freezes well too.

Homemade Curry Paste Tracker

Homemade Yellow Curry Paste Use this section to keep track of the curry batches	
DATE	BATCH NUMBER

Coconut Seafood Curry

COOK TIME
15-20 MIN
PREP TIME
15 MIN
SERVINGS
4-6 SERVINGS

INGREDIENTS

- 2 tablespoons sesame oil
- 1 onion, thinly sliced
- 1 garlic clove, crushed
- 2cm piece ginger, grated
- 2 tablespoons mild curry paste
- 1 tablespoon tomato puree

- 10 prawns, peeled, tails intact
- 1 pound Manila clams, scrubbed and washed
- 2 cans coconut milk
- 1 cup chicken stock
- 2 tablespoons lime juice
- 2 tablespoons chopped coriander leaves

PREPARATION

1. In large mixing bowl combine the following and set aside:
- 2 tablespoons sesame oil
- 1 onion, thinly sliced
- 1 garlic clove, crushed
- 2cm piece ginger, grated
- 2 tablespoons mild curry paste
- 1 tablespoon tomato puree
- 10 prawns, peeled, tails intact

- 1 pound Manila clams, scrubbed and washed

2. Set pressure cooker on High and add the chicken stock and coconut milk and the seafood mixture. Cook on High for 15 minutes. Set timer.

3. Once timer goes off release pressure naturally. Give it a good stir and adjust seasoning to taste, and serve with coriander leaves and lime juice.

Notes

Chicken Squash Carrot Curry

COOK TIME
30 MIN
PREP TIME
15 MIN
SERVINGS
4-6 SERVINGS

INGREDIENTS

- 2 cup brown basmati rice
- Diced chicken breast (add this last)
- 1 tablespoon olive oil
- 1 butternut squash, diced
- 1 red onion, diced
- 2 tablespoon mild curry paste

- 2 cans vegetable stock
- 4 carrots, chopped
- 1 can chickpeas, rinsed and drained
- 3 tablespoon plain Greek yogurt
- Small handful coriander, chopped

PREPARATION

1. Set pressure cooker on High and add all the ingredients into the pressure cooker not including the rice or the coriander or chicken.

2. Cook on High for 25 minutes. Set timer. Once timer goes off release pressure and add the rice into the pressure cooker.

3. Add your diced chicken breasts and a pinch of sea salt and cook on High for another 5 minutes. Set timer.

4. Once timer goes off release pressure naturally and give it a good stir, make sure the chicken is cooked and the squash has softened. Serve with coriander and fresh bread.

Notes

Tamarind Coconut Milk Fish Curry

COOK TIME
15 MIN
PREP TIME
15 MIN
SERVINGS
6 SERVINGS

INGREDIENTS

- 1 ½ pounds haddock (or another mild white fish), cut into pieces
- 2 tablespoons coconut oil, divided
- ½ teaspoon mustard seeds
- 1 onion, diced
- 1 serrano, chopped
- 5 garlic cloves, chopped
- 1 inch ginger, chopped
- ½ cup water

- 1 teaspoon coriander powder
- ½ teaspoon paprika
- ½ teaspoon turmeric
- ½ teaspoon garam masala
- 1 teaspoon salt
- ½ teaspoon tamarind paste
- ½ cup coconut milk
- Chopped cilantro, for garnish

PREPARATION

1. Melt 1 tablespoon of coconut oil in pressure cooker and sauté the mustard seeds. Once the mustard seeds begin to pop, add the onion and serrano pepper. Cook for 8-10 minutes, until the onions begin to brown. Then add the garlic and ginger, stir then turn off heat.

2. Scoop everything out of the pressure cooker and put it into a food processor or blender along with the water. Puree until smooth. Pour this back into pressure cooker add the spices and the fish along with the tamarind paste and coconut milk. Lock lid and cook on High for 15 minutes. Set timer.

3. Once timer goes off, release pressure naturally, give the curry a stir making sure the fish is cooked through.

4. Serve over rice and garnish with cilantro and serve.

Hot Red Fish Curry

COOK TIME
10 MIN
PREP TIME
10 MIN
SERVINGS
4 SERVINGS

INGREDIENTS

- 1 red snapper (or your choice of fish)
- Salt and White Pepper
- ½ cup grated fresh ginger
- 2 tablespoon chili oil
- 1 tablespoon Sesame oil
- 1 tablespoon rice wine
- 1 small onion, diced
- 2 large tomatoes diced
- 1 jalapeño, seeded and diced
- 1 tablespoon olive oil
- ½ cup of honey

For the Red Curry
- 2-3 diced red Thai chili pepper
- 2 cloves minced garlic
- 1 small can of mashed tomatoes
- ½ can of chicken broth
- ½ can of coconut milk
- 1 cup of red curry powder (choose your favorite)
- 1 tablespoon cornstarch + cold water (this is used to thicken the curry only if it's not thick enough)

PREPARATION

1. In a large mixing bowl marinate snapper with the following ingredients then set aside:
- Salt and White Pepper
- ½ cup grated fresh ginger
- 2 tablespoon chili oil
- 1 tablespoon Sesame oil
- 1 tablespoon rice wine

2. In another mixing bowl combine the following and set aside:
- 1 small onion, diced
- 2 large tomatoes diced

- 1 jalapeño, seeded and diced
- 1 tablespoon olive oil
- ½ cup of honey

3. In another mixing bowl whisk together the curry ingredients with wooden spoon:
- 2-3 diced red Thai chili pepper
- 2 cloves minced garlic
- 1 small can of mashed tomatoes
- ½ can of chicken broth
- ½ can of coconut milk
- 1 cup of red curry powder (choose your favorite)

4. Turn your pressure cooker to High and add the curry mixture and bring to a boil then add the onion and tomato mixture from Step 2. Close and lock lid and cook on High for 5 minutes. Set timer.

5. Once timer goes off. Release pressure and add in your snapper mixture. At this point if the curry thickness is not to your like you can add the cornstarch mixture slowly. Or if it's too thick you can add the rest of the chicken broth can.

6. Close and lock lid and cook on High for another 5 minutes. Set timer. Once timer goes off release pressure naturally and serve with fresh green parsley over jasmine rice.

All-in-One Coconut Fish Curry

COOK TIME
25 MIN
PREP TIME
15 MIN
SERVINGS
4-6 SERVINGS

INGREDIENTS

- 4 medium sized filet cod (if frozen, thaw before using)
- 3 tablespoons sesame oil
- 3 tablespoons dark soy
- 2 cloves garlic, minced
- 1 small knob of ginger, minced

- 1 can coconut milk
- 1 can chicken stock
- 1 cup of homemade Curry Paste (See page 82*)
- 50 grams long green string beans, ends trimmed
- 100 grams white cauliflower roughly chopped

PREPARATION

1. In large mixing bowl marinate cod with the following and set aside:
- 3 tablespoons sesame oil
- 3 tablespoons dark soy
- 2 cloves garlic, minced
- 1 small knob of ginger, minced

2. Set pressure cooker on High and add the coconut milk, chicken stock and homemade Yellow Curry Paste and bring to boil, keep stirring. Once boiling add cod filets then add the vegetables. Lock lid and cook on High for 25 minutes. Set timer. Once timer goes off, release pressure naturally and serve with basmati rice or crusty bread.

Tomato Pork Red Curry

COOK TIME
25 MIN
PREP TIME
15 MIN
SERVINGS
4-6 SERVINGS

INGREDIENTS

- 1 pound minced pork
- 3 tablespoons sesame oil
- 1 tablespoon sea salt
- 1 tablespoon white pepper
- 3 tablespoons dark soy
- 2 cloves garlic, minced
- 1 medium purple onion, diced
- 4 large tomatoes, diced

- 1 medium green bell pepper, cut into thin slices
- 1 can coconut milk
- 1 can chicken stock
- 1 cup spicy tomato paste
- ½ cup red curry powder
- ¼ cup ground turmeric
- 2 minced re Thai chili pepper

PREPARATION

1. In large mixing bowl marinate ground pork with dark soy, garlic, salt, and pepper. Set aside.

2. In pressure cooker on High sauté the onion and bell pepper with sesame oil for 5 minutes.

3. Stir in the chicken stock and coconut milk, bring to boil for about a minute then add in the tomatoes, tomato paste, curry powder, turmeric and chili pepper. Stir everything until the powders have incorporated into the liquid.

4. Add the pork mixture give it a good mix, then lock lid and cook on High for 25 minutes. Set timer.

5. Once timer goes off, release pressure naturally, give everything a good stir and serve over jasmine rice or pasta.

White Bean Chicken Chili

COOK TIME
15 MIN
PREP TIME
15 MIN
SERVINGS
6-8 SERVINGS

INGREDIENTS

- 1 pound boneless skinless chicken thighs, cut into 1-inch pieces
- 2 tablespoons sesame oil
- 4 large garlic cloves, chopped
- 1 tablespoon ground cumin
- 1 teaspoon dried oregano
- ½ teaspoon aniseed
- ½ teaspoon dried crushed red pepper

- 1 large onion, chopped
- 3 15-ounce cans cannellini beans (white kidney beans)
- 1 cup canned chicken broth
- 1 7-ounce can diced green chilies
- ½ cup whipping cream
- Grated cheddar cheese
- Chopped fresh cilantro

PREPARATION

1. In mixing bowl season chicken with:
- 2 tablespoons sesame oil
- 4 large garlic cloves, chopped
- 1 tablespoon ground cumin
- 1 teaspoon dried oregano
- ½ teaspoon aniseed
- ½ teaspoon dried crushed red pepper
2. Set it aside let marinate for 5-10 minutes.

3. Preheat pressure cooker on High and add the following:
- 1 large onion, chopped
- 3 15-ounce cans cannellini beans (white kidney beans)

- 1 cup canned chicken broth
- 1 7-ounce can diced green chilies

4. Then stir in your chicken mixture. Lock lid and cook on High for 15 minutes. Set timer. Once timer goes off, release pressure and stir in the whipping cream. Lock lid and cook on High for another 5 minutes. Set timer.

5. Once timer goes off, release pressure naturally and serve over jasmine rice with grated cheddar cheese and fresh cilantro.

Homestyle Chili Con Carne

COOK TIME
10 MIN
PREP TIME
15-20 MIN
SERVINGS
8 SERVINGS

INGREDIENTS

- 1 large onion, diced
- 2 cloves garlic, minced
- 1 pound ground pork or beef
- ¼ cup dark soy sauce
- 1 tablespoon sriracha sauce
- 1 tablespoon chili oil

- 2 teaspoons teaspoon dried oregano leaves
- 2 teaspoon ground cumin
- ½ teaspoon salt
- 1 can diced tomatoes, undrained
- 1 can red kidney beans, undrained
- 1 can beef broth

PREPARATION

1. In a large mixing bowl combine ground pork the following ingredients then set aside:
   - 2 cloves garlic, minced
   - 1 pound ground pork
   - ¼ cup dark soy sauce
   - 1 tablespoon sriracha sauce
   - 1 tablespoon chili oil
   - 2 teaspoons teaspoon dried oregano leaves
   - 2 teaspoon ground cumin
   - ½ teaspoon salt

2. Add the onion, tomatoes, kidney beans and beef broth into pressure cooker, then lock lid and cook on High for 10 minutes. Set timer.

3. Once timer goes off release pressure and add in ground pork mixture, give it a good mix then lock lid and cook on High for another 8 minutes. Set timer.

4. Once timer goes off, release pressure naturally. Stir and serve with crusty bread or toasted tortilla chips.

Chowders

Pastas

Risottos

New England Clam Chowder

COOK TIME
15-20 MIN
PREP TIME
10 MIN
SERVINGS
2-4 SERVINGS

INGREDIENTS

- 12-24 fresh clams (or 11 oz. strained frozen or canned clams)
- 2 cups Clam Juice
- 1 cup, smoked and cured bacon (or pancetta) cubed
- 1 medium onion, finely chopped
- 1 teaspoon sea salt
- ¼ teaspoon pepper
- ½ cup white wine

- 2 Medium Potatoes, cubed skin
- 1 Bay Laurel Leaf
- 1 Sprig Thyme
- 1 pinch, red pepper flakes
- 1 cup milk
- 1 cup cream
- 1 tablespoon butter
- 1 tablespoon flour

PREPARATION

1. Prepare the clams, if fresh was and scrub thoroughly. If canned, drain and set aside.

2. Turn pressure cooker to low and add the bacon sauté until it releases its fat then add the onion, salt and pepper and raise the heat to medium.

3. When the onions have softened, add the wine, clam juice and stir, then add the diced potatoes, bay Leaf, thyme, and cayenne Pepper.

4. Close and lock the lid of the pressure cooker, cook for 15 minutes at high pressure. Set timer.

5. While the potatoes are pressure cooking, make a slurry to thicken the chowder by blending equal amounts of butter and flour over low heat and stirring constantly with a small wooden spoon until they are both well blended.

6. Once timer goes off, release pressure naturally and carefully open lid to add the clam meat, cream, milk and slurry mixture.

7. Stir well, then lock lid and cook on High for another 5 minutes (or until the clams are cooked – shells fully open) Set timer. Once timer goes off, release pressure naturally. Serve with warm bread or soup crackers.

Spicy Lemon Salmon Fettucine

COOK TIME
20 MIN
PREP TIME
15 MIN
SERVINGS
4-6 SERVINGS

INGREDIENTS

- 4 Wild Sockeye Salmon filets
- 2 lemons, juice one and slice the other one
- 2 tablespoons chili pepper powder
- 1 tablespoon chili oil
- Sea Salt, to taste
- Fresh crack pepper, to taste
- 1 cup water

For the Pasta and Herb Butter Sauce

- Cook fettucine to desired firmness for 4-6 servings
- 250 grams of butter partially melted in microwave
- 1 cup fresh spinach leaves, chopped
- 1 tablespoon dried oregano
- 1 tablespoon dried parsley flakes

PREPARATION

1. In a flat plate season salmon with the lemon juice, chili pepper powder, chili oil, salt and pepper.

2. Insert the stainless steel steam rack that comes with your Instant Pot/Pressure Cooker to the bottom of the pot with the handles up, and add the 1 cup of water into the pot.

3. Place the salmon fillets on the steam rack in a single layer and pour any leftover lemon juice and seasoning over the fillets. Cover and lock lid cook on High for 20 minutes. Set timer.

4. While the salmon is cooking prepare your pasta.

5. To make the sauce, in a nonstick skillet add the butter and spinach, cook over medium heat for 1 minute, then add the herbs and combine. Turn off heat and add your cooked fettucine to the skillet and mix well. Season with a pinch of salt and fresh crack pepper. Transfer to plate.

6. Once your Instant Pot timer goes off release pressure and place the salmon filets on top of the pasta and garnish with the lemon slices.

Homemade Enchilada Sauce

COOK TIME
20 MIN
PREP TIME
10 MIN
SERVINGS
4-6 SERVINGS DEPENDING ON YOUR RECIPES

INGREDIENTS

- ¼ cup sesame oil
- 2 tablespoons flour
- ¼ cup red chili powder
- 6 cups of your favorite tomato sauce
- 1 large onion, diced finely

- 2 large tomatoes, diced finely
- 2 cups chicken broth
- ¼ tablespoon ground cumin
- ¼ tablespoon garlic powder
- Salt and pepper to taste

PREPARATION

1. In pressure cooker, add in all the ingredients and give everything a good whisk. Cook on High for 20 minutes. Lock lid and set timer. Once timer goes off, release pressure.

2. Give everything a good stir, check that the tomatoes and onion is very soft and tender, at this point you can either leave the sauce chunky or spoon everything into a blender and blend till smooth.

3. Depending on your preference either chunky or smooth, make sure you portion it into containers and keep frozen for later use. It keeps very well in the fridge up to 2 weeks.

Notes

Turkey Enchilada Rotini

COOK TIME
15-20 MIN
PREP TIME
10 MIN
SERVINGS
4 SERVINGS

INGREDIENTS

- 1 pound ground lean turkey meat
- 1 cup dark soy sauce
- 1 tablespoon dried oregano
- ½ tablespoon dried thyme
- 2 tablespoon white pepper
- 2 tablespoon sesame oil
- 1 tomato, diced
- 1 red bell pepper, diced

- 1 cup sliced cremini mushrooms
- 2 cloves garlic, minced
- 2 cans chicken broth
- 1 cup black olives
- 2 cup freshly shredded jack cheese
- 3 cups homemade enchilada sauce
- 4 cups rotini dry pasta

PREPARATION

1. In large mixing bowl, marinate the turkey grounds with soy sauce, oregano, thyme, and white pepper. Set aside. In pressure cooker sauté on High the mushrooms, tomatoes, bell pepper, and garlic with sesame oil for 5 minutes. Then add in the chicken broth and *homemade enchilada sauce* (**see page 95 for instructions**) and rotini pasta. Give everything a good stir then add in the turkey meat mixture and give it another good stir.

2. Lock lid and cook on High for 20 minutes. Set timer. Once timer goes off, release pressure naturally and give everything a stir and check that the turkey and pasta is cooked.

3. Then mix in the jack cheese and serve with a sprinkle of black olives and a garden salad.

Angel Hair Pasta with Creamed Corn and Peas

COOK TIME
15 MIN
PREP TIME
10 MIN
SERVINGS
2 SERVINGS

INGREDIENTS

- 4 cup frozen corn tidbits
- 2 cups frozen peas
- 2 cloves garlic, minced
- 2 tablespoons sea salt
- 2 tablespoons white pepper

- 2 tablespoon dried parsley flakes
- 2 cans chicken broth
- 2 cups heavy cream
- 3 inches dried angel hair pasta

PREPARATION

1. In pressure cooker, evenly spread out the corn and frozen peas, break the pasta in half (if it's too long to lay flat on the bottom of the pot) lay the pasta over the corn and peas and then evenly sprinkle the salt, pepper and parsley flakes.

2. Add in the chicken broth. The broth should cover everything evenly. Lock lid and cook on High for 10 minutes. Set timer.

3. Once timer goes off, release pressure and give everything a good stir, then add in the heavy cream, stir to combine and then lock lid and cook on High for another 5 minutes. Set timer, once timer goes off, release pressure naturally and serve with your favorite protein.

Notes

Ultimate Turkey Nacho Sauce

COOK TIME
15 MIN
PREP TIME
10 MIN
SERVINGS
6-8 SERVINGS

INGREDIENTS

- 1 pound ground turkey meat
- 2 tablespoon sesame oil
- 2 tablespoon sea salt
- 2 tablespoon crack pepper
- 2 tablespoon thyme
- 2 tablespoon dried parsley flakes
- 1 small onion, diced
- 1 cup finely diced green bell peppers

- 2 jalapeno peppers cut into thin rounds
- ¼ cup lemon zest (save the wedges for garnish)
- ½ cup black olives
- 1 small bunch of cilantro leaves coarsely cut
- 4 cups of chicken broth
- 2 cups grated sharp cheddar
- Sour cream to serve and a bag of your favorite nachos

PREPARATION

1. In a large mixing bowl, mix together the turkey meat with sesame oil, salt, pepper, thyme and parsley. Set aside.

2. In pressure cooker add in the chicken broth and bring to a boil, then add in the onion, bell peppers, jalapeno and black olives. Give everything a stir. Lock lid and cook on High for 5 minutes. Set timer, once timer goes off release pressure and add in your turkey mixture, stir to break apart the meat. Lock lid and cook on High for 12 minutes. Set timer. While it's cooking preheat your oven at 375 F.

3. Once your pressure cooker timer goes off release pressure naturally and stir the meat to break up the larger chunks. Taste the turkey meat sauce and add salt and pepper if needed. In a large baking sheet lay out your nachos, then use a slotted spoon to spoon a layer of the turkey meat over the nachos (try not to use too much of the juice) then add a layer of the sharp cheddar, be generous. Once all the layers are on the baking sheet, pop it in the oven and bake for 5 minutes or until the cheddar is all melted.

4. Serve immediately, garnish it with a sprinkle of the cilantro and lemon zest. Serve with a side of your favorite chowder.

Creamy Potato Cheese Soup

COOK TIME
20 MIN
PREP TIME
10 MIN
SERVINGS
6-8 SERVINGS

INGREDIENTS

- 4 large potatoes, peeled and cut into 1 inch cubes (2 1/2 lbs.)
- 4 small onions, chopped
- 2 teaspoons salt
- 1 ½ cups water
- 4 cups milk

- 1 can chicken stock
- ¼ teaspoon sea salt
- ¼ teaspoon black pepper
- 3 cups cheddar cheese, grated
- 1 tablespoon parsley, chopped

PREPARATION

1. Put potatoes, onions, salt and chicken stock in pressure cooker. Cook on High for 15 minutes. Set timer.

2. Once timer goes off, release pressure naturally and carefully remove lid and allow the potatoes to cool.

3. Spoon the potatoes and liquid into a blender. Blend the mixture smooth and return to pressure cooker.

Add the milk and pepper and cook on High for another 5 minutes. Set timer, once timer goes off release pressure naturally and add cheese and stir till cheese melts.

4. Serve immediately, garnish with parsley and warm dinner rolls.

Notes

Pepperoni Pizza Rigatoni

COOK TIME
20 MIN
PREP TIME
15 MIN
SERVINGS
2-4 SERVINGS

INGREDIENTS

- 16 oz. ground Italian sausage
- 2 tablespoon olive oil
- ½ cup pepperoni, sliced in half
- ½ cup pepperoni for layering
- 4 cups water

- 1 jar Mezzetta Marinara Sauce (use your favorite)
- 2 cups shredded mozzarella cheese
- 3 cups dried rigatoni
- Salt and pepper to taste

PREPARATION

1. In pressure cooker, heat olive oil on High and sauté the ground Italian sausage, until golden brown, then had in the sliced pepperoni.

2. Add in the water and marinara sauce and stir until bubbling. Once bubbling add in the rigatoni, make sure it's spread out evenly. Lock lid and cook on High for 15 minutes. Set timer. Once timer goes off, release pressure naturally and give everything a good stir. Spoon everything into a baking dish and sprinkle with mozzarella and layer the rest of the pepperoni over the rigatoni evenly. Pop it in the oven and boil at 500 F for 5 minutes or until the cheese is melted. Serve immediately.

Notes

Creamy Chicken Alfredo

COOK TIME
20 MIN
PREP TIME
15 MIN
SERVINGS
2 SERVINGS

INGREDIENTS

- 3 tablespoon of olive oil
- 1 small slice of butter for cooking
- 1¼ pounds of boneless, skinless chicken breasts, diced
- 2 cloves of garlic, minced
- 2 tablespoons dried parsley flakes

- 2 cans chicken broth
- 1 cup of heavy cream
- 3 cups of dry penne pasta
- 2 cups of freshly shredded real parmesan cheese
- Salt and pepper to taste
- 1 small bunch chopped parsley leaf

PREPARATION

1. Heat pressure cooker on High and sauté the chicken breasts with butter and olive oil until golden brown. Then add in the penne, chicken broth, garlic, dried parsley flakes and salt and pepper to taste. Lock lid. Cook on High for 15 minutes. Set timer.

2. Once timer goes off release pressure naturally, give the pasta a good stir and stir in the heavy cream. Lock lid and cook on High again for another 5 minutes. Set timer.

3. Once timer goes off release pressure and stir in the parsley leaves and add more salt and pepper to taste.

4. Serve with a garden salad or your favorite chowder.

Notes

Sake Clams and Linguine

COOK TIME
10-15 MIN
PREP TIME
15 MIN
SERVINGS
2 SERVINGS

INGREDIENTS

- 2 pounds Manila clams, scrubbed (try to get them all the same size)
- 2 inches dried linguini, broken in half
- 2 cups halved cherry tomatoes
- 2 tablespoons olive oil
- 1 medium red onion, thinly sliced
- 2 tablespoons sea salt
- 1 tablespoon sesame oil

- 1 cup sake or white wine
- 1 pinch of dried red chili flakes
- 3 cloves garlic, minced
- 4 cups fish stock
- ½ cup chopped fresh parsley leaves
- 1 tablespoon fresh lemon zest
- Fresh lemon wedges to serve

PREPARATION

1. Heat the oil in pressure cooker and sauté the onion with the salt until tender, then add in the garlic and sauté for another 1 minute.

2. Add in the fish stock, linguine, cherry tomatoes, sake, and sesame oil. Spread out the clams over the linguine. Lock lid and cook on High for 10 minutes.

Set timer. Once timer goes off, release pressure naturally and check the pasta for tenderness and that the clams are fully open, it not cook on High for another 2-5 minutes.

3. Serve in shallow plates with fresh parsley, lemon zest and lemon wedges.

Notes

Linguine with Sun-Dried Tomatoes and Brie

COOK TIME
10-15 MIN
PREP TIME
15 MIN
SERVINGS
4 SERVINGS

INGREDIENTS

- 6 inches dried linguine, broken in half
- 1 cup packed fresh basil leaves
- ½ cup sliced oil-packed sun-dried tomatoes
- 3 large garlic cloves, minced
- 4 ½ cups chicken stock
- 2 tablespoons sesame oil

- 2 tablespoon sea salt
- 1 pinch red pepper flakes
- Freshly ground black pepper, to taste
- 8 ounces brie cheese, rind removed and torn into pieces
- Good-quality olive oil, for serving

PREPARATION

1. Combine linguine, basil, roasted sun-dried tomatoes, and garlic into pressure cooker. Add the chicken broth, sesame oil, salt, red pepper flakes, and a generous amount of black pepper and bring to a full rolling boil on High. Then lock lid and cook on High for 10 minutes. Set timer.

2. Once timer goes off, release pressure naturally and use tongs to stir the pasta.

3. Once pasta is at your desired texture then add in the brie and toss with tongs until creamy and melted. Add in the fresh basil and a swirl of olive oil and toss again before serving. Serve with crusty baguettes and garlic butter.

Notes

Creamy Mixed Mushroom Fettucine

COOK TIME
25 MIN
PREP TIME
15 MIN
SERVINGS
4 SERVINGS

INGREDIENTS

- 6 inches dried fettucine, broken in half
- 1/2 cup white mushrooms, sliced
- 1 cup Portobello mushrooms, sliced
- 1 cup cremini mushrooms, sliced
- 2 garlic cloves, minced
- 1 small shallot, minced
- 4 cups chicken stock
- 2 tablespoon sesame oil

- 2 tablespoon sea salt
- 2 tablespoon white pepper
- 2 tablespoon dried oregano
- 2 tablespoon dried parsley flakes
- ½ cup heavy cream
- 250g cream cheese, cut into small cubes
- 1 cup Fresh grated sharp white cheddar

PREPARATION

1. Heat pressure cooker on High and add a swirl of olive oil and sauté all the mushrooms with the garlic and shallot, sea salt, pepper, oregano, and parsley flakes for about 5 minutes.

2. Then add in the chicken stock, and heavy cream. Stir to combine. Then add in the fettucine, lock lid and cook on High for 15 minutes. Set timer. Once timer goes off, release pressure naturally. Add in the cream cheese and mix using tongs, lock lid and cook on High for another 5 minutes. Set timer.

3. Once timer goes off release pressure naturally and fold in the white cheddar into the mushroom fettucine, mix well with tongs and serve immediately with fresh cracked pepper and more sea salt to taste.

Macaroni in a Creamy Lemon Sauce

COOK TIME
1 HOUR 15 MIN
PREP TIME
15 MIN
SERVINGS
8 SERVINGS

INGREDIENTS

- 1 package (16 ounces) macaroni
- 4 cups water
- 2 teaspoons sea salt
- 4 ounces cream cheese, cubed

- 4 ounces shredded white cheese (garnish)
- 1 (12 ounce) can evaporated milk
- 2 tablespoons lemon juice
- 2 tablespoons dried parsley

PREPARATION

1. Mix macaroni, water, and salt together in pressure cooker. Set timer and cook on High for 5 minutes.

2. When timer goes off, release pressure naturally. Then mix in cream cheese and evaporated milk and mix until everything is melted. Simmer the sauce until its smooth and the pasta is at a desired tenderness.

3. Turn off pressure cooker, stir in lemon juice, and dried parsley.

4. Season with additional salt and pepper to taste. Serve with sprinkle of shredded white cheese.

Notes

Cod Fish Chowder

COOK TIME
25 MIN
PREP TIME
10 MIN
SERVINGS
6 SERVINGS

INGREDIENTS

- 2 tablespoon butter
- 1 cup Onion, chopped
- ½ Mushrooms, sliced
- 4 cups Potatoes, peeled & diced
- 4 cups chicken broth
- 2 pounds frozen cod

- 1 tablespoon Old Bay Seasoning (or more)
- Salt & Pepper to taste
- 1 cup clam juice
- ½ cup flour
- 1 cup Half & Half or, 1 can Evaporated Milk

PREPARATION

1. Add all the liquids into pressure cooker first then lay out your frozen cod.

2. Place the potatoes and mushrooms over the cod and add your seasoning. Lock lid and cook on High for 20 minutes. Set timer. Once timer goes off release pressure naturally, and give your chowder a gentle stir breaking up the cod into bite size bits with your wooden spoon.

3. Season to taste and lock lid and cook on High for another 5 minutes. Set timer. Once timer goes off release pressure and serve hot with your favorite dinner rolls.

Notes

Pasta with Meat Sauce

COOK TIME
10 MIN
PREP TIME
5 MIN
SERVINGS
4 SERVINGS

INGREDIENTS

- 1 (32 oz.) jar tomato pasta sauce (store bought or home canned)
- 1 (32 oz.) jar water
- 1 lb. ground meat of choice (turkey, beef, venison or chicken)
- 1 onion, minced

- 1 clove of garlic, minced
- 2 teaspoons sea salt
- 2 teaspoons pepper
- Dash of sriracha
- 2 tablespoon olive oil
- 4 cups pasta of your choice

PREPARATION

1. First brown your ground meat in pressure cooker with olive oil. Once meat is browned add in the rest of the ingredients including the pasta.

2. Set pressure cooker on High and cook for 10 minutes, set timer. Once timer goes off release pressure naturally and check that pasta is at desired softness.

3. Serve hot with a side of garlic bread.

Notes

Hearty Fish Stew

COOK TIME
20 MIN
PREP TIME
15 MIN
SERVINGS
6 SERVINGS

INGREDIENTS

- 2-3 pounds of fresh cod, if frozen, thaw it (you can add frozen baby shrimp too)
- 2 tablespoon sesame oil
- 1 tablespoon white pepper
- 1 tablespoon of salt
- 5 cups of chicken broth

- 1 cup clam juice
- 1 cup heavy cream
- 1 small purple onion diced
- 3 medium size potatoes peeled and diced
- ½ cup white mushroom sliced
- 2 tablespoon dry parsley flakes

PREPARATION

1. In large mixing bowl marinate following and set aside:
- 2-3 pounds of fresh cod
- 2 tablespoon sesame oil
- 1 tablespoon white pepper
- 1 tablespoon of salt

2. Set pressure cooker on High and add the following:
- 5 cups of chicken broth
- 1 cup clam juice
- 1 cup heavy cream
- 1 small purple onion diced
- 3 medium size potatoes peeled and diced and the ½ cup sliced white mushrooms.

3. Bring everything in pressure cooker to a boil for 10 minutes or until potatoes are soft. Set timer.

4. Once timer goes off release pressure naturally and add in your fish mixture and the parsley flakes. Cook on High for another 10 minutes. Set timer. Once timer goes off release pressure naturally.

5. Give it a good stir, if prefer thicker stew add a swirl of flower and cook for another 1-2 minutes.

6. Serve with warm dinner rolls and garden salad.

Winter Vegetable Stew with Barley

COOK TIME
30 MIN
PREP TIME
20 MIN
SERVINGS
6 SERVINGS

INGREDIENTS

- 6 tomatoes, diced
- 2 large carrots, cut into bite size pieces
- 3 potatoes cut into chunks
- 4 celery stalks cut into bite size pieces
- 2 cups of sliced white mushrooms
- 1 large onion, diced
- 6 cups vegetable stock (or beef/chicken stock)

- ½ cup red wine or rice wine (red wine is preferred)
- 1 cup pearl barley
- 3 gloves garlic, minced
- 1 tablespoon dried parsley flakes
- 1 tablespoon dried thyme
- 1 bay leaf

PREPARATION

1. In a nonstick pan add a drizzle of olive oil and quickly sauté the white mushrooms with the minced garlic and onions until golden brown (2-3 minutes on medium heat) then add in the red wine and cook for another minute. Set aside.

2. In pressure cooker add the rest of the ingredients not including the barley. Lock lid and cook on High for 20 minutes. Set timer.

3. Once timer goes off, release pressure naturally and add in the mushrooms and barley, give it a good stir and add a 2 pinches of salt and pepper. Lock lid and cook on High for another 10-15 minutes, set timer.

4. Once timer goes off, at this point the potatoes and carrots should have soften. Add salt and pepper to taste and serve with your favorite pasta dish fresh baked biscuits.

Notes

Cream of Spinach with Chicken Bites

COOK TIME
25 MIN
PREP TIME
20 MIN
SERVINGS
4-6 SERVINGS

PLEASE NOTE: THE RECIPE REQUIRES A BLENDER TO PUREE THE SOUP. THIS SOUP FREEZES VERY WELL. YOU CAN MAKE IT IN LARGE BATCHES AND FREEZE ACCORDING TO DESIRED SERVING SIZE.

INGREDIENTS

- 1 bag of frozen spinach, thawed (If fresh then roughly 4-6 bundles depending on bundle size, some supermarkets carry very large farmer bundles, which you will only need 2 bundles)
- 2 medium size chicken breasts, diced
- 2 cans of chicken stock
- 3 cups of milk

- 3 table spoons of butter
- 1 clove of garlic, minced
- 2 shallots, minced
- ¼ cup flour (only sprinkle if soup not at desired thickness)
- Salt and pepper to taste

PREPARATION

1. Set pressure cooker to High and add the spinach and chicken stock. Lock lid and cook for 15 minutes. Set timer.

2. Meanwhile, in a nonstick skillet add a swirl of olive oil and sauté the diced chicken breasts for 5 minutes on medium then add in the butter, garlic and shallots and sauté for another 5 minutes on high or until meat is fully cooked.

3. Once your pressure cooker timer goes off release pressure naturally and give it a good stir, add in the milk and only add the flour if it's not at desired thickens.

4. Then ladle the spinach soup into blender and blend until incorporated and smooth.

5. Add the soup back into pressure cook along with the chicken. Lock lid and cook on High for another 5 minutes. Set timer. Once timer goes off release pressure. Add salt and pepper to taste and serve with crusty bread and lemon wedges on the side.

Spinach and Artichoke Fettuccine

COOK TIME
15-20 MIN
PREP TIME
10 MIN
SERVINGS
2 SERVINGS

INGREDIENTS

- 2 cups sliced white mushrooms, rinsed
- 1 can artichoke hearts, drained
- 4 cloves garlic, minced
- 2 medium shallots, roughly chopped
- 5 cups chicken broth

- 2 tablespoon sesame oil
- 2 inches of dry fettuccine (measured with hand)
- 1 tablespoon dried oregano
- ½ tablespoon dried thyme
- 1 small bag frozen cut spinach (roughly 14 oz.)

PREPARATION

1. In pressure cooker add in the broth, sesame oil, mushrooms, artichoke hearts, shallots and garlic. Break the fettuccine in half and place on top of the mushrooms and artichoke hearts. Then sprinkle evenly the oregano and time. Add a pinch of salt and pepper.

2. The broth should just about cover all the ingredients, if it doesn't add a little bit more chicken broth. Lock lid cook on High for 10 minutes. Set timer. Once timer goes off release pressure naturally and check the texture of the pasta.

3. Add in your spinach, give it a good stir and lock lid and cook on High for another 5 minutes. Set timer. Once timer goes off, release pressure and if pasta is at desired tenderness, serve in shallow plates with a side of lemon.

Notes

Creamy Coconut Shrimp Udon

COOK TIME
15 MIN
PREP TIME
10 MIN
SERVINGS
2 SERVINGS

INGREDIENTS

- 2-3 packages of udon noodles (not the frozen kind)
- 1 pound of baby shrimp, thawed and rinsed (if frozen)
- 2 tablespoon sea salt
- 2 tablespoon white pepper
- 2 tablespoon dried parsley flakes
- 1 stalk of fresh lemon grass, thinly sliced
- 1 cab coconut milk
- 2 cans of chicken stock

PREPARATION

1. In a large mixing bowl mix together the shrimp with the sea salt, pepper and parsley flakes.

2. In pressure cooker bring to a boil the chicken stock, coconut milk and lemon grass. Whisk for 5 minutes, then add in the shrimp, give it a good stir then add in your packets of udon. Lock lid and cook on High for 10-15 minutes. Set timer. Once timer goes off, release pressure naturally and stir, check to see that undo is cooked.

3. It should be soft and springy. Serve in 2 shallow dish with lime wedges and fresh cracked pepper.

Notes

Tofu Miso Udon Noodle Soup

COOK TIME
10 MIN
PREP TIME
10 MIN
SERVINGS
2 SERVINGS

INGREDIENTS

- 2-3 packages of udon noodles (not the frozen kind)
- 1 box of firm tofu cut into small bite size cubes – smaller the better (found in Asian supermarkets)
- 1 cup of sliced Portobello mushrooms
- ½ cup miso paste

- 3 cans of chicken stock
- 4 cups of water
- 1 tablespoon Shichimi Powder (Japanese chili powder)
- 1 stock of green onion cut into thin slices

PREPARATION

1. Add the chicken stock and water to pressure cook and bring to boil on High, then add the miso paste and mix well with wooden spoon until the paste has dissolved.

2. Add in the Portobello mushrooms and Shichimi powder, give it a mix, and then add in the udon noodles and tofu cubes. Lock lid and cook on High for 10 minutes. Set timer.

3. Once timer goes off, release pressure naturally. Serve in large soup bowls with the fresh green onion slices.

Notes

Tiger Prawn Risotto

COOK TIME
30 MIN
PREP TIME
10 MIN
SERVINGS
2-4 SERVINGS

INGREDIENTS

- ½ pound frozen tiger prawns, thawed and peeled
- 1 teaspoon salt
- 1 teaspoon white pepper
- 3 tablespoons olive oil
- 4 tablespoons butter
- 1 shallot, minced
- 3 cloves garlic, minced

- 2 cups Arborio rice
- ¾ cup cooking sake
- 2 teaspoons soy sauce
- 4 cups fish stock or Japanese Dashi
- 20 grams Parmesan cheese, finely grated
- 2 finely chopped green onion stalks

PREPARATION

1. In mixing bowl season the prawns with salt and white pepper. Set pressure cooker on High and add the olive oil and butter and sauté prawns for 5-10 minutes with the shallot and garlic, the prawns should be about 80% cooked. Remove and set aside.

2. Add the Arborio rice, cooking sake, soy sauce and fish stock into pressure cooker with a swirl of olive oil. Stir and combine, make sure the rice is coated with the liquids. or Japanese Dashi

3. Once timer goes off release pressure naturally and place the prawns on top of the risotto and sprinkle the parmesan cheese over the prawns and risotto. Cover and lock lid again and cook on High for another 5 minutes. Set timer.

4. Once timer goes off release pressure naturally and serve. Garnish with the sliced green onions.

Easy Spinach Lemon Risotto

COOK TIME
20 MIN
PREP TIME
10 MIN
SERVINGS
4 SERVINGS

INGREDIENTS

- 4 packed cups of baby spinach leaves
- 1 tablespoon salt
- 1 tablespoon white pepper
- 4 tablespoons butter
- 1 shallot, minced
- 2 cloves garlic, minced

- 2 cups Arborio rice
- ¾ cup cooking sake
- 4 cups vegetable stock
- ¼ cup cream
- Juice of 1 lemon

PREPARATION

1. In nonstick skillet on medium heat, melt the butter and sauté spinach for 2 minutes with the salt and pepper, shallot and garlic. Set aside.

2. In pressure cooker, add the Arborio rice, cooking sake, vegetable stock, cream and lemon juice. Cook on High for 15 minutes. Set timer.

3. Once timer goes off release pressure naturally and add in the sautéed spinach and give the risotto a quick stir. Lock lid again and cook on High for another 5 minutes. Set timer.

4. Once timer goes off, release pressure naturally and serve with fresh ground pepper along with your favorite meat dish.

Notes

Tomato Lemongrass Risotto with Mussels

COOK TIME
25 MIN
PREP TIME
15 MIN
SERVINGS
6 SERVINGS

INGREDIENTS

- 1 pound of mussels, scrubbed and cleaned
- 1 tablespoon salt
- 1 tablespoon pepper
- 2 tablespoons sesame oil
- 4 tablespoons butter
- 1 large onion, diced

- 2 shallot, minced
- 4 cloves garlic, minced
- 3 cups Arborio rice
- 1 cup cooking sake
- 2 cans of chicken stock
- 1 bunch of fresh cilantro coarsely chopped

PREPARATION

1. In nonstick skillet on medium heat add butter and sauté onion with garlic and shallots, salt, and pepper until tender. Set aside.

2. In pressure cooker add the Arborio rice, cooking sake, chicken stock and sesame oil. Give it a good stir, then lay the mussels over the rice. Cook on High, lock lid and cook for 20 minutes. Set timer.

3. Once timer goes off, release pressure naturally and check that all the mussels have opened fully, add the fresh cilantro and cook for another 5 minutes. Set timer.

4. Once timer goes off, release pressure naturally and serve with a side of lemon wedges and crusty bread.

Notes

Got a Sweet Tooth?

Why not make dessert why your dinner entrees are cooking in your Instant Pot!

These curated desserts are some of my favorite for an after dinner treat. You can make a lot of these desserts ahead of time or while your dinner is cooking in your Instant Pot!

-Jamie Abbott

BAKING COMES FROM THE HEART ♥

The desserts in this collection *do not require* the Instant Pot. You will need to use your oven, mixers, blenders, whisks, etc.

While your dinner is cooking in your pressure cooker, you can make dessert and pop it in the oven.

In the meantime you and your family can enjoy a delicious dinner, and your dessert will be ready after you've finished!

Or you can always make ahead and fill your home with delicious aromas of baked goods.

Cheers.

Raspberry and Cream with Raw Honey

INGREDIENTS

- 2 cups heavy cream, whipped to stiff peaks
- 1 cup raw honey at room temperature
- 2 cups fresh raspberries split between 2 dessert glasses

- 2 teaspoon cinnamon
- Mint leaves for garnish

PREPARATION

1. Divide the raspberries into 2 dessert glasses, drizzle raw honey over the raspberries and add a pinch of cinnamon.

2. Repeat for second glass, then add a dollop of fresh whipped cream and another pitch of cinnamon and garnish with mint leaves. This dessert is great for cleansing your palette after dinner.

This is such a versatile quick and easy dessert recipe that you're whole family would love! The fresh whipped cream should be refrigerated and will keep up to 2 days. You can use the cream in your coffee, tea and other desserts as well. You can also replace the Raspberry with your favorite fruits and for those of you who have a bit of a sweet tooth you can also add chocolate shavings to it!

Notes

Berry Parfait

INGREDIENTS

Simple sheet cake (this is best made night before)
- 4 cups all-purpose flour
- 4 cups packed brown sugar
- ¼ cup baking cocoa
- 1 tablespoon ground cinnamon
- 2 teaspoon baking soda
- 2 cups melted butter
- 1 cup milk
- 1 cup buttermilk
- 2 teaspoon vanilla
- 2 eggs, beaten

For the Parfait
- 2 cups fresh raspberries
- 2 cups fresh blackberries
- 1 cup cool whip or fresh whipped cream

PREPARATION

3. Preheat oven to 350 F grease your sheet cake pan and lightly flour it. In mixing bowl mix flour, sugar, cocoa cinnamon, baking soda, then add butter, milk, buttermilk, vanilla and eggs and whisk until blended.

4. Pour into pan and bake for 40-45 minutes or until toothpick inserted in center comes out clean. Let cool for 30 minutes.

5. Once the sheet cake is cooled cut out small cubes, about a size of a dice. In a tall parfait glass, add a layer of the sheet cake then a layer of cool whip, a layer of the berries and repeat until you reach the top of the class. Top it off with more cool whip and garnish with remaining berries and a dusting of cocoa. Serve immediately.

6. The sheet cake can be divided and stored in freezer for up to 2 weeks.

Notes

Oatmeal Raisin Cookies

INGREDIENTS

- 1 cup raisins (either red or green ones)
- 2 cups Quick oats
- 1 ½ cups All-purpose flour
- ½ teaspoon Baking soda

- 1 cup Butter
- 1 cup packed brown sugar
- 1 Egg
- 1 teaspoon Vanilla

PREPARATION

7. Line 2 baking sheets with parchment and preheat oven to 350 degrees F.

8. In a medium bowl stir oats with raisins, flour and baking soda. Beat Butter with sugar in a large bowl, until fluffy with an electric mixer. Beat in egg and vanilla.

9. Spoon 2 tablespoon portions of dough 3 inches apart onto baking sheets. Flatten them slightly with the back of a spoon. Bake in center rack until edges are golden but centers are soft, bake for 15 min. Transfer cookies to a rack to cool completely.

Notes

Salted Caramel Chocolate Brownie

INGREDIENTS

- ¾ cup plain all-purpose flour
- 1/8 teaspoon Baking powder
- 1 ¼ cups Brown sugar
- 2 Eggs
- 1/3 cup Store-bought caramel filling

- 2 teaspoon Vanilla extract
- 150g Butter melted
- 150g Dark chocolate, chopped
- 1 teaspoon sea salt

PREPARATION

1. Preheat oven to 325 degrees F. Mix the flour, baking powder and sugar in a bowl. Then add the eggs, caramel, vanilla and butter and whisk until smooth.

2. Stir in the chocolate and spoon the mixture deep square brownie dish lined with parchment paper.

3. Sprinkle with the sea salt and bake for 40–45 minutes or until just firm around the edges. Cut into squares and serve warm or cold with vanilla ice cream.

Notes

Banana Cream Pie

INGREDIENTS

- 1 ½ cups Oreo cookie crumbs
- ½ cup Butter melted

Caramel Bananas
- 1 tablespoon Butter
- 2 teaspoon Packed brown sugar
- 2 tablespoon Heavy Cream
- 3 Ripe medium bananas, sliced

Pudding
- 1 ½ cups milk

- 3 tablespoon Granulated sugar
- 3 tablespoon Cornstarch
- 3 Egg yolks
- 1 ½ teaspoon Vanilla

Topping
- 1 cup Heavy Cream
- 2 teaspoon Granulated sugar
- 44 gram bar of Chocolate covered sponge toffee, such as Crunchier, broken into small pieces

PREPARATION

1. Combine cookie crumbs with ½ cup melted Butter mix then press into bottom of a 9-in. pie plate.

2. Melt 1 tablespoon Butter in a medium non-stick sauce pan over medium-high. Add brown sugar, 2 tablespoon Heavy Cream and boil gently, whisking often, 1 min.

3. Remove from heat and let stand 1 min. Stir in bananas, then arrange over crust in an even layer.

4. Heat milk in a medium saucepan over medium-high, just until bubbles form on the surface. Set aside.

5. Then whisk 3 tablespoon sugar with cornstarch and yolks in a medium bowl then whisk in half of hot milk until smooth. Return mixture to saucepan and set over medium. Whisk often until pudding thickens. Remove from heat and stir in vanilla and pour mixture over banana layer, smoothing top. Refrigerate until pudding is set, 1 hour.

6. Beat 1 cup Infused Heavy Cream in a medium bowl until soft peaks form when beaters are lifted, 2 to 3 min. Beat in 2 teaspoon sugar until stiff peaks form when beaters are lifted, about 2 more min. Spoon whipped cream over center of pie.

Chocolate Mousse

INGREDIENTS

- 1½ cups Milk divide portions
- 1 oz. Semi-Sweet Chocolate
- 1 pkg. *Jell-O* Chocolate Fat Free Instant Pudding
- 1 cup plus 2 tablespoon heavy Cream whipped to stiff peaks, divided
- 1/2 cup fresh raspberries

PREPARATION

1. Microwave 1 cup Milk and chocolate in large microwaveable bowl on medium setting for 2 min. whisk until chocolate is melted and mixed. Add remaining milk and dry pudding mix and beat for 2 min. Refrigerate 20 min.

2. Fold in 1 cup of already whipped Heavy Cream.

3. To serve – spoon into wine glasses or dessert bowls. Top with your favorite berries and add another dollop of whipped Heavy Cream.

Yellow Mellow Lemon Pie

INGREDIENTS

- 1 ¼ cups graham crumbs
- ¼ cup butter, melted
- 2 pkg. *Jell-O* Lemon Instant Pudding
- 2 cups milk, cold
- 1 tablespoon lemon juice
- 1 ½ cups heavy Cream divided

PREPARATION

1. Mix graham crumbs and Butter press onto bottom of 9-inch pie plate. Beat dry pudding mixes, Milk and juice with whisk for 2 min. (Pudding will be thick.)

2. Spread 1½ cups onto bottom of crust. Whisk ¾ cup already whipped cream into remaining pudding then spread it over first pudding layer. Top with remaining cream. Refrigerate 3 hours or until firm.

Creamsicle Cheesecake

INGREDIENTS

- 1 cup Honey Maid Graham Crumbs
- ½ cup Butter melted
- 2/3 cup boiling water
- 1 pkg. *Jell-O* No Sugar added Orange Jelly Powder

- 1 cup fat-free cottage cheese
- 1 cup *Philadelphia* Light Cream Cheese Product
- 2 cups Heavy Cream

PREPARATION

1. Mix crumbs with melted Butter they place on bottom of 9-inch spring form pan, press to build a crust. Add boiling water to jelly mix until completely dissolved. Cool 5 min.

2. Pour into blender. Add cottage cheese and cream cheese product. Blend well. Pour into large bowl.

3. Whip Heavy Cream until it forms stiff peaks. Then pour into prepared pan, smoothing the top. Refrigerate 4 hours or until set. Remove rim of pan before serving.

The Red Berry Pie

INGREDIENTS

- 1 cup sugar
- 1 pkg. *Jell-O* Raspberry Jelly Powder
- 2 tablespoon corn starch
- 1 cup water

- 1 baked (9-inch) pie shell, cooled
- 3 cups fresh strawberries, hulled
- 2 cups fresh raspberries
- 1 cup heavy cream whipped

PREPARATION

1. Mix sugar, dry jelly powder and corn starch in medium saucepan. Gradually stir in water. Bring to boil on medium-high heat, stirring constantly.

2. Cook and stir until thickened. Let cool 10 min. Fill pie shell with berries; cover with jelly glaze. Refrigerate 3 hours. Top with whipped cream before serving.

Lemon Poppy Loaf

INGREDIENTS

- 1 ¾ cups All-purpose flour
- 1 cup Granulated sugar
- 1 tablespoon Poppy seeds
- 1 tablespoon Lemon zest
- 1 teaspoon Baking powder
- ½ teaspoon Salt
- ¾ cup butter melted
- 2/3 cup Milk
- 2 Eggs
- 1 teaspoon Vanilla

PREPARATION

1. Preheat oven to 350 F. Oil a 9×5 in. loaf pan.

2. Stir flour with sugar, poppy seeds, lemon zest, baking powder and salt in a small bowl.

3. Beat butter with milk, eggs and vanilla in a large bowl, using an electric mixer on medium, until smooth. Fold in flour mixture until just combined. Don't over-mix. Pour into loaf pan.

4. Bake until a butter knife inserted into center of loaf comes out clean 55 to 65 min. Transfer pan to a rack. Let stand 10 min. Turn out onto rack.

For the Glaze
- ½ cup icing sugar
- 1 tablespoon Lemon juice

5. Whisk icing sugar with lemon juice in a small bowl.

6. Brush glaze over warm loaf. Let stand until loaf is cool, about 2 hours.

Notes

Carrot Cake Cupcake

INGREDIENTS

The Cupcakes

- Paper Cupcake cups
- 1½ cup all-purpose flour
- 1 teaspoon baking powder
- 1 teaspoon baking soda
- 2 teaspoon pumpkin pie spice
- ¼ teaspoon kosher salt
- ½ cup brown sugar
- ¼ cup granulated sugar
- 2 large eggs

- 2 tablespoon fresh orange juice
- ½ lb. carrots, peeled and grated (about 1¾ cups)

The Frosting

- 1 8-ounce package cream cheese, at room temperature
- 1/3 cup sour cream
- ½ cup confectioner's sugar
- ¼ cup Heavy Cream whipped
- 2 tablespoon honey

PREPARATION

1. Heat oven to 425 degrees F. Line 12-cup muffin tin with paper cupcake cups.

2. Meanwhile, in a medium bowl, whisk together the flour, baking powder, baking soda, pumpkin pie spice, and salt.

3. In a large bowl, whisk together the sugars, eggs, and orange juice. Add the flour mixture to the eggs and mix to combine. Fold in the carrots.

4. Divide the batter among the prepared muffin cups.

5. Bake until a wooden pick inserted into the center comes out clean 20 to 25 minutes. Let the cupcakes cool in the pan for 10 minutes, then transfer to a wire rack to cool completely.

6. The frosting, using an electric mixer on low, beat the cream cheese and sour cream to combine. Add the confectioners' sugar and honey and beat until smooth, then fold in already whipped Cream chill until ready to use, at least 45 minutes. Spread the frosting on the cupcakes.

Baked Apple Pie

INGREDIENTS

- 2 ¼ cups flour
- 1 cup shortening
- 5 to 7 tablespoon ice cold water
- 6 cups thinly sliced peeled tart apples (about 4 large apples)
- ¾ cup brown sugar
- ¾ cup white sugar
- 1 tablespoon corn starch
- ½ teaspoon ground cinnamon
- ¼ teaspoon ground nutmeg
- 1 tablespoon lemon juice

PREPARATION

1. Preheat oven to 400 degrees F.

2. Mix flour in large bowl, blend in shortening with pastry blender until mixture resembles coarse crumbs.

3. Add 1 tablespoon of water at a time, mixing lightly with fork until flour mixture is evenly moistened and clings together when pressed into a ball.

4. Divide dough in half. Shape each into ½ in. thick round. Wrap each dough in plastic wrap and refrigerate 10 to 15 min.

5. In a large bowl toss apples with brown and white sugar, corn starch, cinnamon, nutmeg and lemon juice, set aside.

6. Place 1 dough round between 2 large sheets of plastic wrap; roll out dough with rolling pin to flatten slightly, working from center of dough to the edge. Continue rolling until dough round is about 2 in. larger than diameter of inverted 9-in. pie plate.

7. Peel plastic and invert dough into pie plate. Peel off remaining piece of plastic wrap and press evenly. Trim edge with sharp knife.

8. Pour apple mixture into pie plate and cover with the second dough remove plastic wrap and pinch edges together to form ridge. Cut off excess.

9. Cut several slits near center of pie to allow steam to escape. Bake 45 to 50 min. Let Cool and serve with ice cream or whipped cream.

Strawberry Cream Pie

INGREDIENTS

- 1-1/3 cups cookie or graham cracker crumbs (chocolate wafers or gingersnaps work too)
- 6 tablespoon sugar, divided
- 1/3 cup butter melted
- 3 cups frozen whole strawberries, thawed or fresh strawberries if available

- 125 g Brick Cream Cheese, softened
- 2 pkg. *Jell-O* Vanilla Instant Pudding
- 2 cups heavy cream whipped, divided
- Mint leaves or fresh strawberries to garnish

PREPARATION

1. Heat oven to 350 degrees F.

2. Mix crumbs, 2 tablespoon sugar and butter until blended; press onto bottom and up side of 9-inch pie plate. Bake 10 min. let cool.

3. Use pulsing action to process whole strawberries and remaining sugar in food processor just until berries are finely chopped. Add cream cheese; process just until blended. Spoon into large bowl. Add dry pudding mixes; stir 2 min. gently stir in 1-1/2 cups of already whipped heavy cream.

4. Spoon mixture onto crust.

5. Refrigerate 2 hours or until firm. Garnish with remaining whipped cream and sliced strawberries or mint leaves before serving.

Notes

Thank You

We sincerely hope
you enjoyed
cooking with us!

Made in the USA
San Bernardino, CA
06 March 2017